REAL MEMORIES.

AUDIOVISUAL CHALLENGES OF AN
ARCHIVING MUSICOLOGIST IN THE 21ST CENTURY

Gisa Jähnichen

2018

REAL MEMORIES.

AUDIOVISUAL CHALLENGES OF AN ARCHIVING MUSICOLOGIST IN THE 21ST CENTURY

Gisa Jähnichen

2018

Bibliografische Information der Deutschen Nationalbibliothek: Die Deutsche Nationalbibliothek verzeichnet diese Publikation in der Deutschen Nationalbibliografie; detaillierte bibliografische Daten sind im Internet über dnb.dnb.de abrufbar.

Herstellung und Verlag:

BoD – Books on Demand, Norderstedt

ISBN 978-3-7460-6878-7

CONTENTS

REAL MEMORIES…

The collection of articles written by the author in the past two decades shows a lot of issues, developments, and paradoxes that mount up to some "real memories" of virtual documents. Looking back, each of the articles was motivated by a conflict and resulting questions. All articles were trying to answer these core questions or, at least, bring them to public attention. The succession from one perspective to another, from one community to another, also indicates that some problems were grown out by just ignoring them, directly solved by taking action, or by changing conditions through advanced technology.

However, the most sensitive sections of these articles follow the joint approach through the gaze of an observer who is incurably interested in cultural and social aspects of the fact that the accumulation of knowledge through sound and audiovisual documents is crucial to the survival of human communities and their environment. This approach is itself brought up through the conflict between steadily progressing technologies and their application in still slowly learning societies. Finally, the entire sequence of articles leads to rather visionary suggestions that include future models of human life and its ultimate purpose.

The author is a musicologist who by accident started to work in an audiovisual archive while feeling destined for hard core field work in mainland Southeast Asia. Here, as an introduction, the short story is told of how it comes that an archiving musicologist feels audiovisually challenged in the 21st century.

In the early 1990s, shortly after the Berlin wall came down, technology jumped directly into everyone's life and pushed academicians as well as teachers to their limits. The merry old type writer could not be rescued with its electric version though many were happily discarding new tools. For example, I did not dare to own a mobile phone until 2015. However, the early computer era was a field of daily adventures and a huge playground for ways of alternative thinking.

Games, word processing, search engines; all that became a big source of excitement and filled our East-European urban generation with enthusiasm and the feeling of being part of something completely new. The high speed development of video cameras, digital recording systems, and the advancements of mobile notebooks contributed to the never ending fascination. In those times, nothing scared the obsessed and romantic ethnomusicologists keen to use these new things in order to solve old problems.

Political changes were another fact which offered exciting possibilities. The final end of colonial power systems in Southern Africa led my colleague to undertake extensive field work in Namibia, where she got involved in a heavy car accident and passed away. I inherited her rich collection and did not know how to deal with the new possibilities. However, the first step of all, as I learned to think, was archiving the recordings in an appropriate way. As it is part of human history, I tried to let later users decide what to do out of it. I repatriated the collection via the German Ministry of Foreign Affairs and the National Archives of Namibia by transferring a digital copy of the many recordings on different carriers. Also, I got interested in the history of these recordings, the people involved and their lives, the ideas that were brought up by external researchers.

While archiving the sound and audiovisual Namibia collection, the most basic and still applicable principles of archiving emerged. Confronted with all practical and cultural problems in detail and on a daily basis, many pieces fall into their places and de-romanticised the then grown up ethnomusicology which kind of dissolved into cultural anthropology, or just cultural musicology, or later in ecomusicology. This time of intense learning and observing brought me unavoidably into contact with professional organisations and colleagues engaged in this field. I am eternally thankful to everyone who put me on track.

Shortly after that, another large recording and archiving project started in Ho Chi Minh City. This project was again funded by the German Ministry of Foreign Affairs and the local association of composers and musicians. Within two years, the entire repertoire of

desperate enforcement of archiving principles. Later, issues became more complex and academic. The longer I am working in the field of audiovisual archiving the more I am sure of the necessity to convince as much colleagues as possible that they have an obligation in dealing with their audiovisual heritage, their collections, their unwritten material, their orally documented past. And yet, I also learned that not everything can be of the same importance. However, I am sure that future innovations will do much better in making decisions about past achievements. My most urgent goal is in stopping ignorance towards any type of knowledge. That is what drives me and that is what let me feel again like a small and helpless creature in the big world. But one who can change a lot by doing small and seemingly helpful things being an archiving musicologist.

This compilation is thought to provide insights into the learning process and to document some of the many difficulties audiovisual archivists and musicologists face while creating, discovering, and recovering this special kind of human and even non-human knowledge. Audiovisually or just audible memories might be not more real than written chronicles, scientific papers, or academic theses prone to individual re-interpretation. But they are, too, not less real.

Some of the most striking discoveries while being an archiving musicologist is the insight that memorising time must always come with memorising places and agents. In the analogue era, time and place of accessing knowledge in any of the few real audiovisual archives was crucial to development. Now, the exact time, place, and agent of the recorded analogue event is crucial to validate this knowledge and to make any material becoming part of useful data. Another insight was the confirmation that nothing ever is unchanged, that processes are running with different speeds and relative to each other. And the third insight is the simple fact that any archiving musicologist including all their inner struggles is part of the subject, the knowledge source, and the whole experience of life. Real memories always involve present time, place, and every being.

Berlin, January 2018

ACCESSIBILITY OF DIGITALLY BORN INTELLECTUAL PROPERTY: CASES FROM MALAYSIA[1]

INTRODUCTION

As previous experiences show, those who want to consume digital-born Intellectual Property items within Malaysia and abroad do not necessarily know about the why and how of establishing an Intellectual Property status for digital-born knowledge. Many complications arise during the process of establishing and protecting Intellectual Property within a complex cultural environment as that of Asia. One of the key problems is the general gap in understanding what it is that Intellectual Property embraces, and why it is important beyond its primary exploitation for financial gain. Using digitally born examples from Intellectual Property applications sent to Putra Science Park at one of the largest Malaysian Universities within the last three years, this paper illustrates typical complexities that arise in the process of providing access to Intellectual Property-protected items, especially those that attract international interest by companies and individuals who often exploit Intellectual Property from Asian universities.

Taking a central position in this paper is the role audiovisual archivists play in providing secondary access to and preservation of these digitally born Intellectual Property items, beyond their primary uses within the commercial sector. Some contemporary audiovisual content created for commercial and research purposes, especially those created during research with local communities, must endure beyond the Intellectual Property product-development processes of today's profit-minded universities. Audiovisual archivists must be front-and-center in this process, both in selecting and preserving contemporary research output at universities around the world, but also in providing education to communities and researchers around the Intellectual Property process.

---

[1]   First published: Jähnichen, Gisa (2017). Accessibility of Digitally Born Intellectual Property: Cases from Malaysia. *International Journal of Business, Humanities and Technology* 7 (3), 19-24.

1

1. Putra Science Park at University Putra Malaysia

Putra Science Park at Universiti Putra Malaysia, which represents an Asian microcosm of knowledge marketing, is a rich testing ground for researching digital-born Intellectual Property in the context of a variety of information formats, including music and recordings, teaching materials, technology, and graphic design tools. There exists a proper list (figure 1) of types of works and categories which is one of the very few digital items accessible to the public:

NO.	TYPE OF WORKS	CATEGORIES
2.	ARTISTIC	Graphic Photograph Sculpture Collage Work of architecture being a building Model for a building Work of artistic craftsmanship
3.	MUSICAL	Musical works and includes works composed for musical accompaniment
4.	FILM	Being shown as a moving picture -being recorded on other material -the sounds embodied in any sound-track associated with a film
5.	SOUND RECORDINGS	Any fixation of a sequence of sounds or of a representation of sounds capable of being perceived aurally and of being reproduced by any means, but does not include a sound-track associated with a film
6.	BROADCASTS	Transmitting, by wire o wireless means, of visual images, sound or other information which- - is capable of being lawfully received by members of the public - is transmitted for representation to members of the public - includes the transmission of encrypted signals where the means for decrypting are provide to the public by the broad-casting service or with its consent
7.	DERIVATIVE	Translation, Adaptation, Arrangement, other Transformation, Collection of work and Collection of mere data

Figure 1: Table of copyright classification at Putra Science Park, 2016.

The exact wording and the carefulness in filling in this table of possible types of works that can be put under copyright and become an Intellectual Property of the university shows partly in which mood rights are treated in general. We find an administrative copy-paste culture that questions the understanding of the subject matter, for example under the category "musical works". How did this grammatically interesting addition "and includes works composed for musical accompaniment" into this one-point-category? It had to actually being added for the shape of copyright constructions resulting from suggested items that are either inaccessible or not exploitable. Especially in the field of music education and performing arts, the number of such items increases in an alarming fashion. But there are some really positive examples, too: Putra Science Park won a gold award (figure 2) on "Copyright" for a digital born board game for children aged 6 to 12 which was commented on the internal website as follows:

KUALA LUMPUR, Sept 10: Researchers of Universiti Putra Malaysia (Universiti Putra Malaysia) win gold award under the Copyright category during the National Intellectual Property award presentation held in conjunction with 2015 National Intellectual Property Day.

The group of researchers received a trophy, RM10,000 cash [peanuts for the PM], medal and certificate from Prime Minister, Dato' Seri Najib Razak at the Putra World Trade Centre [...] Dr Mohamud Fazli expressed his gratitude for winning the prestigious award...He said 'Professor Bijak Wang' was a board game made locally on financial research which could be beneficial in this era where reports of people going bankrupt were rampant. "This serves as a pro-active step to teach children on financial management, how to go about saving their money, indirectly instilling the culture and habit of saving from a tender age," he said. Prof. Dato' Dr. Mohd Azmi, meanwhile, said... "So far, several established organizations have indicated their interests with the kit and we are in the process of negotiating with them," he said. Universiti Putra Malaysia.

Not surprisingly, this innovation was made during Malaysia's biggest financial scandal in history, the 1MDB issue, in which the Prime Minister seems to be heavily involved which is continuously generating a huge amount of digitally expressed jokes that are not yet copyrighted.'1MDB issue' stands for 1Malaysia Development Berhad Scandal. The Malaysian Prime Minister was accused of taking over RM2.67 billion from a government-run strategic development company in his personal bank accounts. While the game might be indeed a useful idea that was copyrighted for this university, there are quite a number of items that have to be questioned as they infringe other rights due to lack of knowledge in the field and missing networking among a scientific community.

Figure 2: Award presentation held in conjunction with 2015 National Intellectual Property Day in Kuala Lumpur, Malaysia, Dr. Mohamad Fazli receiving his award from Prime Minister Najib Razak at the Putra World Trade Centre. Photo: courtesy of Saleha Haron.

2. FOOLS

Among them are the following digitally born Intellectual Property items that do not look digital at the first view. For example the performance of an electric violin in upside down position hanging at a rope and flying through the performance hall (figure 3). The video

4

taken through a mobile phone device was sufficient in order to prove the uniqueness of the event and the individual effort.

Figure 3: Photo of the event, performance of an electric violin in upside down position, taken by Yktang Photography for public promotion and used as cover photo in social media.

However, the performance style was not new (Pink did it before and it became a fashion over the years); the music was simply played back, and the mobile phone video was anything but an art work so far. A former colleague who is in the field of popular music and digital culture and was not even briefly consulted comments: 'According to my observation in Chinese Pop for years, Taiwan's Jolin Tsai (蔡依林) is the first to integrate gymnastics into live dance & music performance. She earned massive attention for her "perseverance" and effort to take real training in yoga and gymnastics as a pop artiste. (Chow Ow Wei, 2016). This Intellectual Property item caused confusion as other staff were told to start playing their instruments in silly positions for the sake of the Key Performance Indicator of the Department, the Faculty, and subsequently the university ranking. A number of other interesting items could be taken as Intellectual Property coming from the same source. There was even an entire music CD recorded in a private home studio of the staff consisting of merely re-arrangements of oldies such as *Simple Gifts, Miserlou, Greensleeves, Danny Boy* and

5

some others that are now kept as "compositions". This music composition Intellectual Property item was celebrated over months with a large banner at the university entrance. It came even under a specific knowledge class. After intervention by other universities, two things happened: A further specification was introduced which is "Type", that was then filled in as "Arrangement"; and access to these entries was restricted to the own university staff only.

Despite this memorable item were many other Intellectual Property recordings of short snippets that had to be timely stretched though the performer played just a few minutes in a concert one or two short music pieces composed and arranged by others in order to allow for an administratively measurable importance (Minimum of 20 Minutes). The whole list applicable for Intellectual Property items is provided on a burnt CD and a write up that had to be defended in front of a board of experts mostly consisting of the director of Putra Science Park or her vice director, one staff working in humanities and one lawyer. There is no expertise on recordings, on archiving, on music, on performance, or anything near to it. No reviews are undertaken, no input from external experts asked for. The proving material, at the end, is then stored in a normal office building on a normal shelf among many other folders and papers, mostly under temporary air conditioning during office hours. This example encourages many other colleagues to do the same and to put their karaoke sessions which means teaching lessons with power point text running over the screen as Intellectual Property items in order to satisfy quantitative standards. And this is multiplied with all universities in Malaysia and possibly other places where quantitative competitiveness is a core business. The items declared Intellectual Property, as it is understood, are not for re-use or application. They are just numbers. And they can actually only be accessed by the creators or owners, which is Universiti Putra Malaysia staff or staff of the respective research unit. But there is another contradictory issue which is the true creation of knowledge that takes part at any university. Among those items that really could have an impact on knowledge increase are recordings of teaching processes in performance studies and consecutive unique lesson plans as well as true compositions for locally available performers. These recordings cannot and should never be stored under the conditions given by Putra Science Park or any similar institution anywhere else in the region. The good news: they are rarely stored under such conditions. The bad news: they are often not stored at all.

3. COUNTER MOVEMENT

While building up the music department's own Audiovisual Research Collection for Performing Arts as a small scale university archive, it was impossible to co-operate with Putra Science Park in terms of archiving issues. The only approval was given for the database, a digital document developed for onsite use in the most effective and simple way. This database is continuously updated. However, the recordings need to have a back-up on the university server that is not included in this Intellectual Property process though it was included in the write-up. This safety copy storage was subject to completely other negotiations among IT staff that were well aware of the risks that digital items include. But these negotiations had nothing to do with Intellectual Property rights issues. The university is actually not interested in doing anything out of them as there is little understanding of items that cannot be listed as single 'events' commodities on a carrier. On the other side, the digital policy of the university prescribes full entries of teaching and lesson plans with uploading of all teaching material, digital sound and video recordings included. These items are supposedly covered by the employment contract and owned by the university without a clear Intellectual Property declaration and they consist of not a few illegally downloaded material, therefore access to them is strictly limited to Universiti Putra Malaysia staff.

"With regards to intellectual property rights in the universities, workers are employees of the university and the law provides that if an employee has created an intellectual property in the course of employment, the university as an employer owns the intellectual property, unless there is a contract at the beginning of the period of employment stating otherwise. The legal position is clear to every type of intellectual property." (Ramli et al, 2016, 1226).

The crucial point is whether an artwork or anything that could be an Intellectual Property item was created "in course of employment". Does free time and holidays count into the course of employment? Is it legal to use university properties while creating artworks but then claiming Intellectual Property privately, for example sitting in the office chewing on an office pencil and dropping some dots on a music sheet? Why staff has to declare Intellectual Property officially if otherwise everything is owned by the university? Where is the motivation for the staff to further create Intellectual Property items? To clarify: Intellectual Property declaration has – as the previous discussion shows – little or nothing to do with knowledge building or protection. In performing arts and performing arts education, it is additionally accompanied by lack of understanding its core business such as the identification of unique performance values, whether musically or performance-wise. In humanities with very few exceptions it is sadly enough not even a primarily economic value but a symbolic value that increases countable items for a better result in university rankings.

4.1. DEMOTIVATION

Instead of doing research that needs a lot of preparation, administration, discipline, and networking, especially performing arts staff opts often for a shortcut in putting some extra-university performances recorded with whatever was at hand and declare it as Intellectual Property. According to the author's observation, out of 14 IP items counted in a time period over three years 2012-2014, 12 were just recorded extra-university activities in events with many performers that were not reviewed regarding quality, copyright issues, and/or length of performance. The main problem of all these interwoven causalities is the problem of accessibility. Intellectual Property items stored at a central university unit that consist mainly sound and audiovisual recordings are actually in-accessible to learners and teachers unless an economic interest is uttered and these items are approached as a commercial user. Interestingly, even though Intellectual Property items created automatically through the contract policy of the universities cannot be re-used internally without this formal commercial intent. Only the marketing department of the university is allowed to access items for free and/or at any time. And it is all too well known how many audiovisual experts, performing arts experts, or even AV archivists are working in university marketing departments: Zero. This answers the earlier question of how comes this odd addition into the list of copyright categories "and works composed for musical accompaniment". Unsure whether something is composed or just re-arranged, a work of music or a work of acrobatics, for accompaniment of whatever show, dinner, celebration, or high tea, everything can be in the inaccessible stock of Intellectual Property items.

4.2. MOTIVATION

And there is the backside of the ranking medal: Those IT staff and dedicated archivists who are truly interested not only in keeping digitally born Intellectual Property but in the very essentials of their knowledge contribution care about present decisions and their consequences for the future. As far as possible and with the consent of the Intellectual Property creators, official university Intellectual Property items and 'normal' audiovisual items which are simply stating copyright (considering project bound items as Universiti Putra Malaysia legal status) that can be archived in the on-site audiovisual archive to ensure their further existence beyond the lifespan of a CD or DVD being stored on an office bookshelf with an on-off air condition environment. The main point, however, is to also ensure accessibility in long term, even if they are temporarily restricted, of all items that might be not in the scope of the Intellectual Property marketing departments.

Another interesting point is that commercial interest in audiovisual items that might be university Intellectual Property seems to increase with the inaccessibility. The pro-active role audiovisual archivists play in providing secondary access to and preservation of these digitally born Intellectual Property items, beyond their primary uses within the commercial sector, is crucial to the social task of the university (figure 4).

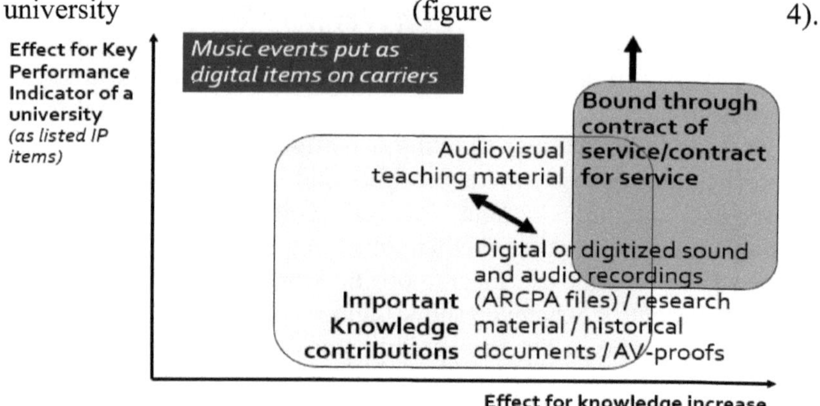

Figure 4: Overview about processes and proportions from the perspective of 'university units versus knowledge creators'. The more 'useless' the item the better for the KPI. The more important for the main university task of building knowledge and teaching, the harder to be acknowledged as this is fixed through contract of/for service.

Some contemporary audiovisual content created for commercial and research purposes, especially those created during research with local communities, must endure beyond the Intellectual Property product-development processes of today's profit-minded universities. Audiovisual archivists must be front-and-center in this process, both in selecting and preserving contemporary research output at universities around the world, but also in providing education to communities and researchers around the Intellectual Property process. This educational task connected to archival work is again a crucial undertaking in societies that struggle hard in overcoming of postcolonial nationalism, of devaluating art as subordinated commercial tool, and of ideological or religious resentment against core disciplines of social sciences such as history, geography, anthropology, philosophy, and the arts. Interestingly, the avoidance of anything entertaining in circles of the religious policy is often being instrumentalised by staff in performing arts when questions are asked about restricted access or potential re-use of any of the named items. It is said that administrators are biased in taking these items in the list after they know the contents. They will restrict access and avoid re-use that is, however, exactly what is wanted by the creators of this type of Intellectual Property items. Everyone gets some points and nobody is harmed.

5. OUTLOOK

These conditions then have to meet with administrative practicalities regarding Intellectual Property establishment from staff, contract regulations, and the distribution of competencies and power. Ramli et al who described parts of the latter problem based on a comparison between research universities in Malaysia conclude that "The university's intellectual property policy must also provide guidelines on the allocation of university intellectual property ownership provided that the policy is legally valid to bind members of the university." (Ramli et al, 2016, p. 1252).As many of the project work and substantial knowledge accumulation is realized by temporary contract staff, this might become a major problem in the future of many large Asian universities, as could be explained taking the example of Malaysia.

REFERENCES

1MDB issue (n.d.). http://www.wsj.com/specialcoverage/malaysia-controversy; last visited 22 April, 2017.

Chow Ow Wei (2015). Personal Communication about footage from 2006: https://m.youtube.com/watch? v=9f cX GGvNF2I.
Last visited 22 April, 2017.

Maimunah, A. (2011). Malaysian Industrial Relations and Employment Law, Kuala Lumpur: McGraw Hill Education.

Ramli, N., Zainol, Z. A. and Tengku Zainuddin T. N.A, (2016). Ownership Rights to University Invention: Universities Legal Authority to Exert Ownership Interest or Claim. Pertanika J. Soc. Sci. & Hum. 24 (3): 1241 - 1252.

Universiti Kebangsaan Malaysia (2010). UKM Intellectual Property Policy 2010.Bangi: UKM Press.

University of Malaya (2010). Intellectual Property Policy for University of Malaya.UM Centre of Innovation and Commercialization UMCIC.

University of Western Australia v Gray (No 20) [2008] FCA 498.

Universiti Putra Malaysia (2007). Universiti Putra Malaysia Research Policy. Retrieved from http://www.upm.edu.my/ dokumen Universiti Putra Malaysia_Research_Policy.pdf.

Universiti Sains Malaysia (2009). Universiti Sains Malaysia Intellectual Property Policy. Research and Innovation Division, USM.

Universiti Teknologi Malaysia (1999). Intellectual Property Policy Universiti Teknologi Malaysia. Research and Management Centre, UTM.

Zakaria, Azman (2015). UPM sweeps gold in Copyright category at National Intellectual Property Award. http:// www.upm.edu.my/news/upm_sweeps_gold_in_copyright_ca tegory_at_national_intellectual_property_award-25156?L=en. Last retrieved 22 April, 2017.

AUDIOVISUAL KNOWLEDGE MANAGEMENT AND THE FEAR TO LOSE CONTROL[2]

In the past, knowledge of any kind was long time monopolized by a few high ranking persons of a community. Since technology enabled people of all social layers in nearly all regions of the world, the problem of monopolization is increasingly repressed. However, cultural diversity in dealing with knowledge and its status is still reflected in societal behaviour and reproduces historical conditions regarding audiovisual archiving even now.

This paper is to introduce the process of implementing a small scale university AV archive and the many contradictory issues in dealing with it as a working tool, as a knowledge property, as a place of higher or lower levels of safety and as the troublesome memory of academic fallacies.

In a critical review, the way keywords and basic bias work is described as well as its effect on the implementation process. In result, an open strategy is proposed to identify culturally determined perspectives in distinction from individual understandings in this matter. The material used is collected through a two year university project at Universiti Putra Malaysia and subsequent discussions.

Not even 100 years ago, in many cases the only person of the village who had a 'vision' was the shaman. He could see what others could not. The shaman was said to be the seer and the hearer of the outer world. His power depended on this belief nurtured through common people's interpretation. Anything the shaman uttered was taken seriously. In other places, religious leaders, respected monks, those who could read and write were an alternative source of knowledge

---

[2] First published: Jähnichen, Gisa (2015). Audiovisual Knowledge Management and the Fear to Lose Control. *IASA Journal, 45*, 54-58.

beyond the daily life experience. However, the monopoly on knowledge was well confined to persons who derived their power from it.

2. ONE CASE

I just had an insightful talk with one student who submitted an interesting paper to a book series we publish annually. His main subject is a video production of two minutes and two seconds length, a musical parody on a university incident that was put on YouTube and richly commented on by Malaysian netizens. In order to provide the reader with full details, he asked the video producer for permission to include this video into the audiovisual supplements coming with each number of the book series. The producer not only allowed him to use his video, but he also sent him a high-resolution version in order to secure the best possible quality for publication. The student then asked me how to do in-text references of this video and I recommended him to archive the video first in order to use the unique archive code as reference in addition to the name such as "([name of video producer], ARCPA 3821)". In the videography he has to provide the full reference and give sufficient acknowledgments as usually required for the database of the archive.

The student hesitated. His argument was that he did not let the author know about being archived, so the author may object to it. He found it unethical to proceed without informing the donor and asking for consent regarding this 'new' or 'different' situation and he somehow felt that he could not ask him for that. Further he found it unethical of me to ask him directly, since that would imply doing something behind the author's back.

We had the following conversation:

- Do you think that the author believes we can control all people who will buy the book?

- No, but that is fine. He knows that the book will be sold.

- What is the difference between being 'out of control' on the book market and being archived with unaltered rights and acknowledgements in an archive that can control access onsite?

- It is that the author does not know it. I should ask for his permission again.

- Do you know that anyone who buys the book with the AV supplement can archive the files stored on the DVD for safety reason on another carrier? I will have to do it after publication as well in order to ensure the safety and accessibility of the files in case ofre-prints or re-editions. That is my duty as an editor.

- But that is unethical!

- I feel that it is unethical to keep a file sent to you for the purpose of publication and subsequently 'uncontrollable' distribution on your private computer thus making any further developments depending on you.

- But I was the one who asked him to send it and he sent it to me. He trusts in me.

- So, if you feel responsible for the wellbeing of the file, you should archive it. And if you think that this is unethical, you may restrict access for onsite view only. But then you should ask the author whether he agrees with this restriction.

- Hm. [I have to think about that.]

- This twist of argumentation is typical for the small university AV archive project, called

- Audiovisual Research Collections for Performing Arts (ARCPA).

3. Knowledge Management as Theory

ARCPA was started in 2011 when a group of researchers at the Faculty of Human Ecology of Universiti Putra Malaysia took up an explorative research project on the feasibility and the impact on research and creative art works of a small scale audiovisual archive within the faculty's music department   Two years later, the archive was installed as a "one site entry and access archive" equipped with all playback units necessary for digitization and dependable networking supported through the university as the storage provider. Since the project started, 14 archiving persons, mostly the collectors themselves, registered 69 different recording persons with 28 different declarations of legal status. To date, 2,576 entries have been made and more than 3,000 items from other archives or storage departments have been deposited for unrestricted onsite access. The archive is used by many students and some staff as well as by outsiders to the university.

ARCPA is operated by temporary users such as graduate students, visiting researchers, and staff in order to increase the physical safety of their recordings and teaching materials and to document the legal status of works jointly produced with musicians, performers, and colleagues in the field. Database entries are created and maintained by the main collectors themselves under the guidance of a voluntary archivist on duty. Copyright and legal status or resulting claims are not altered through the archiving process.

Most of the audiovisual documents belong to university grant funded projects and are therefore controlled legally by the university. However, the main agents, the recorded musicians and performers, are the primary copyright holders. The main collectors, mostly the project leaders, but also the primary copyright holders, may restrict access to documents for certain purposes or persons.

However, the archive strives for long-term accessibility since the main idea is to re-use and to effectively exploit existing audiovisual documents for research and educational purposes.

4. FEAR IN REALITY

Fighting with highly sensitive issues caused through culturally different approaches to archiving and access, the archive cannot yet be seen as a safe place for knowledge management.

Coming back to the example given above: What does the story of the student's query imply?

- Archiving is more dangerous and uncontrollable than publishing. (You may ask somebody to be published but not to be archived.)

- Archivists can do worse things with archived items than publishers.

- Accessibility of an archive is unlimited through file duplications while publishers may just stop publishing the item, then it will not be distributed anymore.

- Archives deal with rights differently than publishers.

- The purpose of archiving remains unclear and unforeseeable.

- An archive is like an evidence room of the court; things cannot easily be put in or removed.

- Therefore, they are not flexible and can become a hindrance in development.

- While agreeing on publication, the publisher will bear a part of responsibility, but in an archive things are not transparent regarding responsibilities. No one knows what could happen in the future.

If we put this list of statements into a table and include two columns — the suspected danger for being part of a book publication and the same for being included in and AV archive — and rate them on a scale from 1–5, then we come to this result:

Risk	Being part of a book publication	AV Archiving	Unpublished and stored on home PC hard drive	
			As expected	In reality
Uncontrollable	5	1	1	5
Not to be trusted	3	3	1	3
Access can't be stopped	5	1	1	1
Insecure legal rights	3	1	1	5
Unclear and unforeseeable purpose	1	1	1	3
not flexible, hindrance in development	5	1	1	3
not transparent regarding responsibilities	1	1	1	5
Risk (the higher the number the higher the risk)	23	9	7	25

Figure 1: Open survey on perceived risk levels being considered by archiving students and staff in humanities (January 2015, UPM, 38 participants).

The fear of losing control seems to be widely irrational. However, AV archives have to struggle with this irrationality that is culturally patterned and cannot be reduced to simple misunderstandings.

Another example can illustrate even better which nature of fear we have to deal with and what could possibly cause it.

5. OTHER CASES

On 15 June 2013, a group of researchers attended a recording session in a Malay wedding and an evening rehearsal. The musicians called themselves Nobat Nafiri Melaka. One of the researchers intended to write a thesis about these musicians, the others were asked to help with the recordings. While the wedding went on, the music performed was taken from a broad traditional entertainment repertoire re-arranged by the Nobat Nafiri musicians. The evening rehearsal was mainly to instruct younger musicians in traditional court music pieces that have to be learned entirely by heart. The place for the rehearsal was outside the state Melaka for some special reason. Since Melaka has no court and no Sultan or any other state representative besides the elected governor, court music cannot be played in Melaka. The musicians, who all live and work in other serious professions in Melaka, especially in Kampung Cina, have to go to the neighbouring state Negeri Sembilan in order to play court music. The rehearsal house is attached to a piece of land owned by a relative. The rehearsal takes place only in the darkness.

The house consisting of one room, where the instruments are stored and an attached terrace with roof, where the musicians sit and play, is also a meeting point for villagers nearby who come in search of advice and cures. Besides the rehearsal house, there is another one-room house on stilts, where cooking utensils and construction materials are stored. This house is also used for so called bomoh activities, healing rituals that are conducted by the eldest Nobat Nafiri member. The recordings were brought to the university archive and documented. A set of copies was taken by the researcher who is writing his thesis. Since then, nothing happened.

No thesis is written yet and no access should be given unless this occurs. However, another member of the recording team mentioned in a public meeting the fact of having heard a Melaka Nobat Nafiri group and was harshly criticized. Since Melaka has no court there cannot exist any Nobat group. Later, the researcher who was writing his thesis took this incident as a reason to decline his enthusiasm by saying that his research data were stolen and openly distributed thus his writing would not be of unique value anymore. The data collected and the knowledge retained seemed to go nowhere.

And another example of frustration is the entire collection of a very famous Malay storyteller, Said Aripin, unfortunately also one of the last of his kind. He was the first to have performed in London's Albert Hall as one of those people of public importance that were invited to Great Britain after proclaiming the independence of Malaya. The storytelling was conducted on university ground during three nights with private technical support and some small funding for recording material and catering. The text of the sung stories was later transcribed in a handwritten manuscript by a student who voluntarily wanted to help the head of the department.

Since then, seven years ago, nothing has happened. The manuscript was not even typed into a computer in order to support the documentation. It is also privately secured and inaccessible.

Nobody can do research on it unless a financed project is approved. Students are discouraged to listen to the recordings and any further discussion is stopped.

These two cases illustrate the tragic patterns behind the activities. Knowing that only audiovisual archiving can secure an important part of any performance practice 111, technical equipment and knowhow are very much asked for. Once the 'items' — recordings — are created, the interest in them declines rapidly. The items seem to become suddenly troublesome and a burden for the administration. They are quickly stored away as 'project outcomes' and 'research reports'. While owning items is widely accepted and obviously presented as research achievement, sharing is seen as unethical because sharing is considered as a matter of personal attachment to the items that can only be exchanged between intimate friends. Any other free sharing for the sake of increasing wisdom on a subject is a sort of betrayal.

6. CONCLUSION

Analysing the three cases presented here, we can summarize that knowledge, as something

to live and to grow through sharing, is not an appreciated value in the currently practiced academic culture of Peninsular Malaysia. Knowledge is widely seen as an asset in personal promotion and an achievement assigned to its owner, in this case of the audiovisual 'items.' Therefore, audiovisual items cannot be simply included in an archive and if so, not simply be accessed unless the owner — actually the one who was responsible for conducting an approved and financed research programme — agrees graciously upon it.

The real situation of acknowledging rights in documentations and references does not change this situation, because the power of a project leader is mainly based on dependencies of co-researchers, mostly graduate students or colleagues of lower rank. The power balance decides finally whether a collection can be used successfully.

Culturally, this situation is still far from what audiovisual archiving might be in other areas of the world.

Interestingly, among the musicians recorded, the people who help in arranging sessions and meetings with performers in the communities are much less affected by academic considerations of power relations. They are very often disappointed by not becoming known through archiving activities and by not being included in the discussion of resulting knowledge. However, even if we state certain sociophobic behaviour, conducting AV archiving in a Malaysian university seems to be a long term undertaking in terms of determination and stubbornness. Every year a challenge, every teaching hour a very small step into an open minded world in which knowledge cannot be monopolized or hidden, in which knowledge invites creative spirits to contribute without hesitation.

The hesitation and the way of hiding is the result of social condemnation, the many years in which knowing things or having seen things could be only powerful in the hands of a few leaders and otherwise quite harmful. The remaining distortion derives from barely movable academic structures and a working design that affects all types of knowledge, not only knowledge that comes with AV documents.

REFERENCES

Jähnichen, Gisa (2014). The Right to Know and the Right to Be Known. Paper presented at the *International Colloquium on Music Research 2014 "Music: Ethics and the Community"*. Universiti Putra Malaysia.

Jähnichen, Gisa and Ahmad Faudzi Musib (2013). Social Scientists as Users: Searching for Recorded Sound in its Environment: Cases from Borneo. *IASA Journal, 40*, 44-54.

Jähnichen, Gisa and Chinthaka Meddegoda, eds. (2013). *(Music + Dance) Envirnoment.* UPM Book Series on Music Research, 5. Serdang: UPM Press.

Massey, Rachel, and Christopher Stephens (1998). Intellectual Property Rights, the Law and Indigenous People's Art. *UNESCO Copyright Bulletin 32(4).*

Mills, Sherylle (1996). Indigenous Music and the Law: An Analysis of National and International Legislation. *Yearbook for Traditional Music, 28,* 57-86.

Musib, Ahmad Faudzi, Gisa Jähnichen and Chinthaka Prageeth Meddegoda (2014). The Audiovisual Research Collection for Performing Arts (ARCPA) at Universiti Putra Malaysia: Negotiating Ethical Issues in Social Sciences. *IASA Journal, 43,* 53-59.

Seeger, Anthony (1996). Ethnomusicologists, Archives, Professional Organizations, and the Shifting Ethics of Intellectual Property. *Yearbook for Traditional Music, 28,* 87-105.

Willinsky, John (2009). *The Access Principle. The Case for Open Access to Research and Scholarship.* Cambridge: MIT Press.

THE RIGHT TO KNOW AND THE RIGHT TO BE KNOWN[3]

If X writes an article about Y and publishes this article with publisher Z, nobody will be surprised that all of them agree upon that finally a book with this article is on the public market and subsequently on a bookshelf in private houses and libraries enriching the amount of knowledge and opinions on the subject matter. That is obviously the very aim of writing and publishing. If X records sound or video of Y and puts this recording in an archive, things seem to be different. What causes the difference? A special quality of the negotiated item? A special legal situation? Special ethic issues of the community?

This paper tries to clarify the understanding and processing of knowledge provided through unconventional formats such as digital audiovisual recordings, depictions and metadata mainly used in academic research on music and sound. The discussion will focus on the complexity of philosophical thoughts on current developments and some contradictory issues found within the media market and the academic world. Observations made within the framework of a two year project at Universiti Putra Malaysia, examples from the Phonogram Archives in Vienna, Berlin, St. Petersburg and the Archives of Traditional Music in Laos will serve as examples in providing an overview of considerations to be made while dealing with audibly and/or audio-visually accessible knowledge.

This study is structured in order to examine the relationship between various types of rights in the context of rapid changes in technology and subsequent attitudes towards knowledge and the ethical dimension of their application. At the end, popular misconceptions

---

[3] First published: Jähnichen, Gisa (2015). The Right to Know and the Right to Be Known. *Music: Ethics and the Community*. Edited by Gisa Jähnichen, Made Mantle Hood and Chinthaka Prageeth Meddegoda. *UPM Book Series on Music Research, vol. 7*. Serdang: UPM Press, 209-226.

about knowledge, professionalism, and audiovisual archives will be addressed.

***

During my professional life, I have recorded more than 8.000 audiovisual items. All of them are archived in designated audiovisual archives of different size and affiliation such as the Berlin Phonogrammarchiv, the Phonogram Archive Vienna, the National Archives of Vietnam, Switzerland and Namibia, but also small, specialized archives in Laos, Portugal and Malaysia. Only a very small amount of fresh recordings are still to be processed since fieldwork is steadily on going. I grant free access to all items and request only direct re-confirmation in the case of commercial use. This happened, however, only seven times and all requests were satisfied within days for mutual benefit such as a donation to the archive that maintains the recordings. I was twice heavily plagiarized, mostly regarding additional documents, which were not my main focus. Problems arising from it could be quickly solved without calling upon authorities. Also, I experienced plagiarism in that context as accidental carelessness rather than an intentional crime. Actually, I was somehow happy that somebody wanted to make use of it. None of these cases had a clear commercial background. It was institutional creativity of websites and only in the second instance thoughtless copying.

However, experiences like that do not stop me from collecting, archiving and giving access. They just refine my way of making data base entries. I enjoy feedback and discussion on items and related metadata and I invite colleagues, scholars, and students around the world to explore them in order to maximize their usage and potential.

A completely different perspective on rights connected to collecting audiovisual data and their future was observed recently when I found myself in the situation during fieldwork where I was equipped with high standard recording tools, I observed relatives and friends of active participants recording a music session or explanation about it on their mobile phones at nearly the same time I did. A few days later, these recordings were presented on an internet platform, while my own recordings were still being processed and properly archived. One week later, while sitting in front of the data base computer, I was already affected by the feedback traceable on that internet platform and I included a part of this experience into my description.

RIGHTS IN THE CONTEXT OF RAPIDLY CHANGING TECHNOLOGY AND ATTITUDES TOWARD KNOWLEDGE

The example shows very clearly how some slowly evolving considerations resulting from academics dealing with modern communication technology, distribution of knowledge and the modified awareness of copyright issues are getting rapidly outdated in the moment they are just being written down and discussed in a conference.

Before getting into details of some examples, I want to review a few ideas of Seeger's inspiring article on 'Intellectual Property and Audiovisual Archives and Collections'.[4] This article is 13 years old. However, it appears as if it was written yesterday, since many observations can be made today and many attitudes towards audiovisual archives and collections have not changed.

Seeger sighs about the current situation: "Most archives, in particular, find themselves in the position of a horse being kicked forward and reined in at the same time [...]. Faced with the tremendous challenges of preserving disintegrating collections, prodded by increasingly entrepreneurial administrations to be more self-supporting, kicked by patrons for not having more online, and reined in by concerns about copyright and ethical uses of their materials, archivists rarely buck, but we do roll our eyes in frustration, consider other jobs, and may forget what we have learned

---

[4] Seeger, Anthony (2001). Intellectual Property and Audiovisual Archives and Collections. Folk Heritage Collections in Crisis. *Council of Library and Information Resources Report, May, 2001*. http://www.clir.org/pubs/reports/pub96/contents.html.

through decades of work with our collections, with depositors, with patrons, and with communities" (Seeger, 2001: 1).

The well expressed confusions and resulting insights in how complex and at the same time how contradictory different stakeholders of sound and audiovisual archives act towards knowledge creation, preservation and distribution are based on a few basic misunderstandings on copyright issues and ethical considerations that will be examined below.

Further, Seeger distinguishes between library collections of published material and unpublished material mainly collected through field work, concert recordings or research activities. This distinction is maintained in this study.

A very crucial precondition for a discussion on preserving rights concerns the recorded performing artists: "To transfer rights, the artist must possess the rights to the performance, which may not always be the case" (Seeger, 2001: 3). Without this precondition, a discussion of further applications of rights is without substantiation.[5] Therefore, here are only examples discussed, in which recorded persons were able to co-operate as creators or co-creators of the audiovisual items.

Also, Seeger's notice that any "...discussion of copyright law must be placed in the context of the societies in which the currently observed laws were developed" is vital to the topic. He recommends that

---

[5] For example, cover songs of actual hits performed during a university contest in Malaysia are performed without legislation since the artists did not obtain the rights of the performance nor did the event organizer, which is usually responsible for it in order to organize the event, in this case regulated by the Public Performance Malaysia (PPM), a licensing body for music reproduction in the whole country including institutions of higher education or the Music Authors' Copyright Protection Berhad (MACP), an organisation that deals with live performances accordingly. Therefore, the artists cannot transfer any rights of the performance to somebody else. These recordings cannot be archived or exploited for promotion. Though this is widely practiced, it is an ethical issue that should be considered at least in the context of teaching music advocacy.

copyright law "should be seen as the production of a specific group of people in specific societies at a particular moment in their histories" (ibid.)[6]. Taking all these well-expressed considerations as a starting point, some issues are investigated next.

RIGHT AND COPYRIGHT ON INTANGIBLE ITEMS THAT DO NOT GENERATE INCOME

While giving examples on copyright issues, most of the time (Ammann, 2000; Brown, 1998) the final outcome of the story is an unfair generation of income by those who had the ostensible right to do so but should feel guilty about it. Nevertheless, the copyright applied allows for this since any copyright is not made for ethical considerations. That means that something can be based on a given 'right' but can be, at the same time, unethical and vice versa. Therefore, the outcry for justice does not touch the actual set of laws: it addresses the ethical principles backing the existing copyright law or the ethical principles in which copyright law, however outdated, is applied. Seeger's article calls for cultural consideration and for revision of law sets on copyright (Seeger, 1992, 1996, 2001). In continuation of this attempt, I propose a change to this perspective and a revision of ethical justifications that lead to copyright as a law set and its infringement.

In the following section is demonstrated how ethical considerations of performances become subordinated to copyright issues through an initial establishing of rights that did not exist before. This initial action starts a process that is hard to stop later. It causes a number of

---

[6] They were "developed and codified in Europe and the United States and have become the framework for international intellectual property law". At another places he says that "After a fixed period, copyright material would enter the public domain and become available to anyone for making copies or using in other forms. This is an important part of copyright and patent law: the restrictions are temporary to enable the creator to benefit from the creation and after a fixed time the restrictions expire so that the public may benefit from the free flow of information.

ethical confusions and may lead – from the perspective of audiovisual archiving – to a re-thinking of geography with regard to audiovisual recordings and their features as commodities.

The South African publication, 'Southern Times', reports "Music Publishers took the Belgian tenor, Helmut Lotti to court, the tenor argued that he had done nothing wrong by using the late Miriam Makeba's songs among the Click song and that they were traditional materials. But the Belgian court dismissed Lotti's claims." [7] In defence, Lotti argued that all the material he had used was in the public domain and as such nobody had a right to them. He claimed that the songs in question were all African traditional songs. And he is correct so far.

Miriam Makeba's Click Song is indeed traditional as she is confirming it. However, when still in the public domain, RCA Victor (LSP:2267, Track 3, 2:09') recorded the song in 1960 as "Folk" and transferred the rights to the publishing company. The song was a pure vocal song without further arrangement that might have been copyrighted. Since then, the copyright law set works on the company's side. Going back to the very basics as stated by Seeger, that you can only transfer a right if you own it, the first infringement – if any – is done by Miriam Makeba herself when she was transferring the right of the song to the company since she could not own the song. She was merely the performer and the recording company may own the technical recording but not the song. Rationally, a song that cannot be owned by anybody according to existing copyright law sets cannot be owned by another individual either (Brown, 1998). Subsequently, nobody infringed the copyright and even Helmut Lotti is not wrong or as wrong as anybody else in the history of the song.

---

[7] Helmut Lotti's real name is Helmut Barthold Johannes Alma Lotigiers. He is a Belgian tenor.African traditional music open to abuse, The Southern Times, March 2014, online edition.

http://www.southerntimesafrica.com/news_article.php?id=7879&title=Af rican%20traditional%20music%20open%20to%20abuse#.UyO_Rc6Dk1 5, last retrieved 10 March 2014.

This case offers a lot of thinking about the sense and nonsense in application of copyright law sets not considering cultural diversity in ethical approaches. Copyright law sets which put the individuality of the creator historically derived from copyright law sets developed for written publication and publishing houses do not take into consideration groups of people who may own an intangible asset such as music or special knowledge. The weak point is, therefore, that individuals may create a right out of something that was unrestricted and not previously subject to income generation. By becoming an income generating item, the question of rights turn to produce an unfair treatment in the view of the 'creators', the group of people to which this item may belong. It could be further discussed whether this unfair treatment is tolerated by the creators and only felt by the observers who take an ethical perspective informed by a wider discourse.

Global mobility and intercultural exchanges do not contribute much to 'locate' a group of righteous owners; nonetheless, an appropriate way of respect towards the source of music and knowledge should be maintained. Only after the 27 guaranteed years of copyright ownership, in 1989, the song's 'copyright went to the Paris based African company "Disques Espérance", which does not yet mean that the song was 'freed' from its copyright burden by reaching its approximate source locality. The once non-existent right was transferred many times, split up and transformed into something different since record companies change their owners and their affiliation more or less in the same way as any other commodity.

Title (Format)	Label	Catalogue Number	Country	Year
Miriam Makeba (LP, Album, Mono)	RCA Victor, RCA Victor	LPM 2267, LPM-2267	US	1960
Miriam Makeba (LP)	RCA Victor	LSP-2267	US	1960
Miriam Makeba (LP, Album, Mono)	London Records, London Records	HA 2332, HA.2332	UK	1960
Miriam Makeba (LP, Mono)	RCA Victor	LPM 2267	Canada	1960
Miriam Makeba (LP, Album)	London Records	115.201	France	1963
Miriam Makeba (LP)	London Records	GL 1808	UK	1966
Miriam Makeba (LP, Album, RE)	RCA Camden	CDS 1068	UK	1970
Miriam Makeba (LP, Album, RE)	RCA	CDS 1068 (LSP 2267)	UK	1970
Myriam Makeba (CD, Album)	Disques Espérance	CD 5564	Africa	1989

Figure 1: This table shows successive publishing of the Click song recording made by RCA Victor and the final geographical shift. On the other hand, the table hides the shifts and splitting of ownership.

Disques Espérance

Profile:	French label based in Paris, specialized on world music in general and African music in particular. Part of Sonodisc.
Sublabel:	Prestige de la musique extraeuropéenne
Parent Label:	Sonodisc
Sites:	disquesesperance.com, sonodisc.net

Sonodisc

Profile:	Paris based African, Caribean and World music label. Now owned by Jean Karakos (From Celluloid Records). Also own the sub labels Disques Esperance, African and Suave
Sublabels:	Africa Oumba, African, AfroVision Records, Al Sur, Disques Espérance, Disques Vacances, Fiesta Records, GD Productions, Ozileka, Publi-Congo, Sonafric, TG Sawa, Voice Of Lebanon
Sites:	sonodisc.net

Figure 2: In 2014, Disques Espérance was a sub-label of Sonodisc owned by Jean Karakos. Geographical shift and label naming provide an illusion of spatial contexts in order to divert potential customers. However, the recording made in 1960 is now owned by Sonodisc. In times of disappearing music practices, a recording of this considerable age becomes an even more valuable asset.

CHALLENGES OF ETHICAL JUSTIFICATIONS IN AUDIOVISUAL ARCHIVES

Audiovisual archives around the world have to deal with these elementary problems in various ways. An audiovisual archive's main material are recordings that do not generate income, however, one or other item may be of commercial interest, mainly in the context of promotion for exotic goods and foods as well as travel destinations (Ammann, 2000). Put into percentage, these cases are very rare, especially in research archives, in which generating income is definitely not the main focus. Research archives generate research data and documents that serve as references and indicate a status similar to "publications" if unrestricted access is given. Many data and documents, however, are restricted for various reasons. Some of them for very good reasons such as those restricted recordings of rituals or related events that deal with taboos.[8] As far as these restrictions are temporary (Seeger, 2001), the archiving process, maintenance and documentation is motivating. Less motivating is the oversight of not changing the restriction after reasons for restrictions became obsolescent; such as the research outcomes on supposedly rare audiovisually supported findings are already published. By failing to lift restrictions, the value of the printed publication may decrease through inaccessible references. Who may believe in descriptions of something that cannot be traced?

In academic research, referencing is one of the most basic tools in establishing credibility. Why should audiovisual documents be

---

[8] As shown in an article on the Sebbang of the Bidayuh (Jähnichen & Frank, 2015).

excluded from this principle? Despite these cases that can be found in large unspecialized archives serving a wide range of research institutions, the more frustrating cases are those where audiovisual data are created and explored but inaccessible even to a restricted group of users though the users might be the main stakeholders in a music or sound research project.[9] Research data and audiovisual documents unavailable for references create an increasing cost factor for funding organizations and demotivate researchers who are forced to repeat recordings or to ignore previous findings through lacking audiovisual references. Again, the generation of income is widely negligible, however, the generation of academic reputation and subsequent income or academic 'safety' within a research institution is of importance to collectors, recordists or performers. Focusing on audiovisual archiving from this perspective, the misconception of copyright law sets and their universal application is a triviality. In the context of academic ethics and knowledge distribution, restrictions are highly counter-productive, especially when considering the involvement of different users and contributors who may also have various goals in dealing with audiovisual documents. All of them like to know them, additionally, most of them like to be known as contributors. In the creation of audiovisual documents, institutional hierarchies are ineffective since pure copyright principles have to be applied. Thus, for example, a leader of a research unit cannot function as copyright holder if he or she was not really practically involved in it as recordist or performer.

PRACTICAL ISSUES OF RIGHTS IN THE WORK FLOW OF AUDIOVISUAL ARCHIVING

Audiovisual archiving may resemble the following workflow: X records video of Y. X holds the rights of the recordist (a sub-category within one set of copyrights for the entire item). Y holds at

---

[9] These types of overly protected researches are reminiscent of the middle ages, when monasteries protected their secret magic formulae against ghosts and evils in order to stay in power over a large territory.

least the right of the performer (another sub-category). Y may also hold the primary copyright of the contents if Y created the contents. If Y performs an item of the public domain or anything which is placed apart the applicable copyright system such as traditional music or dance, Y does not hold the copyright of the contents as well as X does not obtain the main copyright on the content. The final recording, which means the physical item derived from the intangible performance, is copyrighted by the institution, in many cases the funding organization, or the legal person, if conducted privately, that initiated and enabled the recording. Though there have been other serious restrictions through missing proofs on copyright of the recordists. However, if these elementary negotiations have been conducted in a proper way as prescribed through national rules, the institutional copyright or the individual copyright could be stated for the recordings. Nevertheless, the right of the technical recording that is the subject of research data and documentation does not include the right to the content, which is intangible and has to be fully transferred from the creating person or persons if full copyright wants to be stated.

Z, the archive, will not touch any of the rights notified if the archive is a facility with a well thought code of ethics. Only special permission is given to make a safety copy in order to ensure the physical existence of the carrier. Hence the carrier is owned by the archive, the rights connected to any information on it are not altered.

Since performer Y cannot realize any long lasting income from holding rights merely on the performance, only recognition is given through notifying the performer's right of Y. It is the right of Y to be known and to be recognized through documentation that might be temporarily restricted in access but generally tangible.

Figure 3a and b: Gonder 1997; Kuching 2009. Multiple rights can derive from these visuals, however, the question of copyright and how it affects the use of these visuals is only discussed when an income can be realized. (Photos by the author).

Many recordings in large archives are sparsely equipped with proper recognition of performer's rights[10], especially older recordings or recordings made by researchers who are informed by the way of data collection represented through older recordings. Even partly illegally produced audiovisual media such as CDs, VCDs and DVDs, do not provide sufficient documentation on the performers that include place and time, name and other identifiable information. One can read, especially in some older recordings, for example: "African folk song performed by women", or "Flute playing by the Kammu in Northwest Vietnam", or "Ritual text of the Lao Sun". This might have been due to little importance granted the performers, or due to the publishing quality. However, in both cases the performer's rights were not appropriately acknowledged.

Recordists are better off since they are mostly those who provide the recordings and the more or less complete information to the archives (Schüller, 2008). They will rarely forget to put their names. Over this, they may forget that there would not have been anything to record without the performers, who also have names and who are also creative.

---

[10] Phonogram Archives in Vienna, Berlin, Petersburg and Bruxelles.

Arriving at the second decade of the 21st century, the world of knowledge faces many contradictions. First and foremost, cultural misconceptions are transformed into global rule sets and affect local networks because traditional knowledge is not valued, since the creation of new items from publicly accessible sources is preferred. For example, musicians playing traditional music may feel 'colonised', badly treated and exempted from success (Jabbour, 1983). Therefore, recordings made with people that are working with traditional music or knowledge in any place of the world deliberately bring them into the context of an art market that looks for rights in producing marketable items. The definition of success, nevertheless, derives from the same law set as the copyright, which values individuality before joint group action in creative arts and which points mainly towards generating income. [11] This perspective contradicts in many ways the social function and cultural understanding of performing arts (Willinsky, 2009, Mills, 1996, Massey & Stephens, 1998).

However, the current situation regarding collecting, preserving, maintaining, and giving access to audiovisual recordings with the aim of generating income is challenged through the following facts:

The available technical infrastructure is not anymore required from publishing companies since recording equipment and know how are widely affordable and accessible.

Rights deriving from the ownership of infrastructural tools are obsolete since outcomes of recording sessions can be collected, preserved, maintained and distributed in many different ways independent from superior infrastructure providers such as archives, museums, universities, ministries and others.

---

[11] Richmond points out that from these contradictions derive conflicts of interests in music education (Richmond, 1996:14).

Rights deriving from preceding knowledge that was once accessible only to a group of selected persons are no longer relevant since most of the relevant expert knowledge is widely accessible, despite the fact that true expertise is declining in result of difficulties in economically justifying them in the framework of superior infrastructure providers such as archives, museums, universities, ministries and others.

Rights deriving from institutional attachment are obsolete since the authority of scholarship and research does not solely depend on affiliations. Contents experts working in a real independent working environment may become an extinct species.

However, that also means that all advantages in obtaining, processing and distributing audiovisual recordings through advanced technologies and shifts in interdependencies are at the same time disadvantages seen from the perspective of generating income. The high pressure through oversupply of once highly interesting and rare audiovisual recordings leads to an increasing indifference concerning professionalising in performing arts. This development affects strongly the entire attitude toward musicianship and its preservation thus the outcome of rights' creation might be the dissolution of the content or at least of the part that is meaningful to the community. And this seems to be the real danger in the process. Are there alternatives that could prevent stagnation on the side of the producers and the final users?

Figure 4: Copyleft sign, one of many movements based on a creative dealing with copyright

Copyleft, a movement based on a creative dealing with copyright is viral. It is constructed on allowing various degrees of use, distribution and modification of any copyright item with the condition that derived works follow the same law set of copyleft.

This wonderful idea first realized by Richard Stallman in the GNU project[12], nonetheless, has again the existence of a "work" as a precondition that would allow for the establishment of copyright. This weak point of copyleft is currently worked out by mainly internet engineers and pioneers in the field of open access movements. Though in the last 20 years many alternative projects were successfully implemented such as Creative Commons and others, a clear line is not yet found that could be applied globally. There are various movements in some countries to free audiovisual material from restrictions in the context of education and sciences. The ratification and the enforcement are dependent upon good will. On the other hand, users still distrust unconventional patterns of using material that is obviously owned by someone else. One can find, therefore, researchers repeating field recordings or pulling out their own equipment in front of another recording team to ensure the ownership status of their work.

MISCONCEPTIONS ON DEPOSIT AND PUBLIC AVAILABILITY OF AUDIOVISUAL RECORDINGS

Another issue important to audiovisual archives, especially to small scale research focused archives in the field of performing arts, is to answer a long list of questions deriving from common misconceptions that are connected to the special quality of the archived items as being sound or audiovisuals.

Here is a list of the most common misconceptions that were discovered while conducting a research project that aimed at proving an increasing effectiveness of an audiovisual archive for performing arts for musicological research at the Universiti Putra Malaysia funded by the university itself. Here is a list of common misconceptions confirmed through earlier observations made in other audiovisual archives.

---

[12] General public license applied on illustrations and adds, but also on software.

- By publishing any type of material in an openly accessible systems, I make myself vulnerable since I can also cause openly accessible reviews of my work. I do not want to be criticized.[13]
- By publishing any type of material in openly accessible systems, I ease the way of plagiarism. I do not want to be plagiarized.
- By transferring data into an audiovisual archive, I cannot ensure being the first to use the archived material for scientific analysis. Therefore, others have to wait until I come up with my research, even if it takes me 10 years.
- By transferring data into an audiovisual archive, I declare the amount and the quality of the collection (a number of items belonging to any type of subject such as a research project, an event, a set of interviews on a topic and many others). I do not want everybody knowing that.
- By transferring data into an audiovisual archive, I lose control of where these data go. I want to control them.
- I feel burdened with archiving and actually I do not want to make data accessible in order to avoid later explanations and eventually resulting responsibilities.

---

[13] Cort and Bishop who investigated into the research culture of social scientists, add up to this list from their observations: "…archiving is seen to be associated with a managerialist and audit culture that has begun to pervade higher education in recent decades, and that it will place an additional administrative burden on researchers unless a commensurate level of resources is provided to assist with this process."…"The second unarticulated concern among qualitative researchers is the possibility that depositing their data for others to access will open up their research practices to surveillance and criticism. Since intellectual critique and debate are a core feature of the advancement of knowledge, this hesitation among qualitative researchers is not a sign of any general unwillingness to submit their ideas or methods to external validation. Instead, it derives from their view of qualitative research as a personal endeavour – largely due to the significant personal and emotional involvement of the researcher in the construction of data (including interactions with research participants and general conduct in the field) – and a corresponding fear that others may scrutinise something so personal and declare it inferior." (Cort & Bishop, 2005).

- Nobody paid me for gathering the data. Why should I make it accessible for free? The archive may make a business out of it without letting me know.
- I do not want others to use my data that I collected with many personal efforts for creating their research outcomes in a cheap way. Then they get the credits, and I am in the shadow.
- Archiving is generally useless. For what do we need to keep all these byproducts?
- In addition to these common misconceptions there were other rather particular misconceptions observed such as:
- Qualitative data as constructed data include researchers' bias and therefore they are highly interpretive. Without the researcher's guidance, the data do not make sense to others. I do not have time to always be there.
- Research areas are personally attached to a researcher through investment of time, personal interaction and subsequent reputation. I do not want to fight with competitors in my field.
- I need to know and like the archivist(s) personally in order to trust in their sensibility towards my feelings on archived materials. The archivists should always be on 'my' side.
- I have to protect third parties who may not agree to be archived since I do not have their legal statement. I do not want to get into trouble.
- I do not want to embarrass any relatives who were involved in producing data and may associate this time with tense feelings.

In the following table, possible responses are listed in support of a modern knowledge society with alternative possibilities:

By publishing any type of material in openly accessible systems, I make myself vulnerable since I can cause also openly accessible reviews of my work. I do not want to be	Then one should also avoid publishing articles or books, since critical exchange, feedback and corrections are part of an academic life.

criticized.

By publishing any type of material in openly accessible systems, I ease the way of plagiarism. I do not want to be plagiarized.	Plagiarism is not caused through accessibility. No publishing house or archive can ever exclude that accessible documents are unlawfully copied. However, the person who is plagiarizing is fully responsible since that is the wrongdoing person, not the publisher/archivist.
By transferring data into an audiovisual archive, I cannot ensure being the first of using the archived material for scientific analysis. Therefore, others have to wait until I come up with my research, even if it takes me 10 years.	Restrictions are only temporary useful, however, they depend on applicable copyright law sets. In most cases, restricting access touches the right to be known, thus others' rights might be infringed.
By transferring data into an audiovisual archive, I declare the amount and the quality of the collection (a number of items belonging to any type of subject such as a research project, an event, a set of interviews on a topic and many others). I do not want everybody knowing that.	The openly declared amount and quality of any collection is part of research credibility. Additionally, not using other's collections in preparation might be seen as a lack of knowledge in the field. Archiving is giving and taking for the sake of knowledge.
By transferring data into an audiovisual archive, I lose control of where these data go. I want to control them.	That happens to any article or book written and no scholar is surprised about it.
I feel burdened with archiving	That might be a question of

and actually I do not want to make data accessible in order to avoid later explanations and eventually resulting responsibilities.	truthfulness in the way of obtaining the data. Explanations might be only avoided through accessibility.
Nobody paid me for gathering the data. Why should I make it accessible for free? The archive may make a business out of it without letting me know.	There is no research archive that makes an income out of its main task. However, an archive has expenses that have to be covered. The value is higher physical safety and legal recognition. On the other hand, the archive is also open to the complaining researcher. How much knowledge a researcher could gain without collecting data him/herself? Also, the costs are already paid. By not using material, it will not become cheaper. It will only become more useless.
I do not want that others use my data that I collected with many personal efforts for creating their research outcomes in a cheap way. Then they get the credits, and I am in the shadow.	This can be avoided through proper documentation. Again, archiving is giving and taking.
Archiving is generally useless. For what keeping all that byproducts?	And for what writing about all these byproducts?

Figure 5. List of possible responses in support of a modern knowledge society.

THE RIGHT TO KNOW VERSUS THE RIGHT TO BE KNOWN?

Rights and ethical considerations that may back them are in many ways contradictory. However, the right to know and the right to be known do not necessarily oppose each other. Drafting a framework for the establishment of rights is the crucial point of departure for further dealing with copyright issues. Since copyright is a culturally patterned condition that includes a historically grown understanding of material and materiality, copyright should always be set into its actual cultural context, which is now characterized by rapidly changing technology and attitudes toward knowledge. The global aspect and the local attitudes are subject to these changes as well as the individual in the centre of it. Following the strict distinction of archived material, right and copyright on intangible items that do not generate income are the main concern of audiovisual archives dealing with research matters. Keeping this in mind, the task in these archives is preserving and maintaining the content of the collections, but law sets and commercial practice may harm the living musical practice that is to be preserved through supporting recordings. That leads to challenges of ethical justifications in audiovisual archives. As practical issues of rights in the work flow of audiovisual archiving demonstrate, accelerated changes in technology and the opening of large consumer markets for any tools and know how in archiving processes offer many advantages that may be seen as democratization, however, the attitude toward knowledge management is affected since the market participants will have to focus on generating income from sound and audiovisual recordings and will not care about items that do not generate income. Contents expertise may expire soon.

Lastly but not unimportantly, a number of common and particular misconceptions on deposit and public availability of audiovisual recordings exist that are hard to overcome, especially in regions where rapid changes in technology have taken over in a very short time and are not based on a long term adaptation to meaningful applications toward knowledge preservation. Re-thinking these misconceptions, another right appears: the right not to be known, which is currently vividly discussed in mainly industrialized regions.

It draws on alarming signs of uncontrollable distribution of privacy information. Unethical practices in this area are widely ignored by state institutions and cause an increasing discomfort leading to dropouts from knowledge networks, social media and in some cases even from life. This topic, however, needs much more space for discussion than offered through this study. However, all aspects discussed so far point toward the fact that ethical consideration in the framework of rights and law frameworks need far more cultural expertise and call for increasing efforts to compensate qualification gaps through high-speed technology development. At this point it is good to return to Seeger who comments:

> "As a scholar I have been humbled by the significance of some of the by-products of the research of anthropologists and folklorists. One hundred years after their publication, few articles in the Journal of American Folklore or the American Anthropologist are of more than minor interest. The recordings made by some of those authors, however, often continue to be very exciting to scholars, musicians, and members of the communities in which they were recorded. Over time, it may be the collections we have made rather than what we have done with them for which we are most gratefully remembered. This requires many of us to rethink our priorities and pay attention to the fate of our recordings, photographs, and unpublished materials" (Seeger, 2001: 9).

Concluding this very rough, snapshot-like overview about the issues of rights in audiovisual archiving processes and connected academic development, the question arises whether a discussion of rights and the ethical principles backing them might still be appropriate (Edmondson, 2004). In academic institutions focusing on a high quantity of academic output regardless of its social impact (Leydesdorff, 2006), the maintenance of all types of knowledge sources might be questioned. Another picture opens up only when starting to turn the perspective into a direction that has the impact on life quality, the expansion of knowledge and its application as well as the humane fairness in recognizing creativity as being part of the meaning of life in its centre. In the right to know and the right to be known, we are all equal. The right to restrict, to avoid and to hide is a sign of a counter-productive academic policy that will ultimately question the sense of science.

REFERENCES

Ammann, Raymond (2000). *The Archive Works of the Vanuatu Cultural Centre to Preserve and Maintain Melanesian Music.* Paper presented at the conference "100 Years of the Berlin Phonogramm-Archiv" in Berlin, October 2000.

Brown, Michael F. (1998). Can Culture be Copyrighted? *Current Anthropology 19* (2), 193–222.

Cort, Louise and Libby Bishop (2005). Strategies in Teaching Secondary Analysis of Qualitative Data. *Forum: Qualitative Social Research, 6* (1), 1–23.

Edmondson, R. (2004). *Audiovisual Archiving: Philosophy and Principles.* Paris: UNESCO, Information Society Division.

Jabbour, Alan (1983). Folklore Protection and National Patrimony: Developments and Dilemmas in the Legal Protection of Folklore. *Copyright Bulletin* 17(1), 10–14.

Jähnichen, Gisa & Beddie Frank (2015). The Bidayuh's Scbbang: Preservation Issues. Music: Ethics and the Community. Edited by Gisa Jähnichen, Made Mantle Hood and Chinthaka Prageeth Meddegoda. UPM Book Series on Music Research, vol. 7. Serdang: UPM Press, 175-184.

Leydesdorff, L. (2006*). Mapping Interdisciplinarity at the Interfaces between the Science Citation Index and the Social Science Citation Index.* http://www.leydesdorff.net/sci _sosci/index. htm, last retrieved 2 October, 2010.

Massey, Rachel, and Christopher Stephens (1998). Intellectual Property Rights, the Law and Indigenous People's Art. *UNESCO Copyright Bulletin 32* (4).

Mills, Sherylle (1996). Indigenous Music and the Law: An Analysis of National and International Legislation. *Yearbook for Traditional Music 28*, 57–86.

Richmond, John W. (1996). Ethics and the Philosophy of Music Education. *Journal of Aesthetic Education*, 30 (3) (Autumn, 1996), 3–22.

Schüller, D. (2008), *Audiovisual research collections and their preservation.* Amsterdam: European Commission on Preservation and Access.

Seeger, Anthony (2001). Intellectual Property and Audiovisual Archives and Collections. Folk Heritage Collections in Crisis. *Council of Library and Information Resources Report, May, 2001.* http://www.clir.org/pubs/reports/pub96/contents.html.

Seeger, Anthony (1992). Ethnomusicology and Music Law. *Ethnomusicology 36* (3), 345–360.

Seeger, Anthony (1996). Ethnomusicologists, Archives, Professional Organizations, and the Shifting Ethics of Intellectual Property. *Yearbook for Traditional Music 28*, 87–105.

Willinsky, John (2009). *The Access Principle. The Case for Open Access to Research and Scholarship.* Cambridge: MIT Press.

Turning Audiovisual Archives into Scientific Assets[14]

University practice requires a high level output of publications and other evidence of scholarly productivity by its researchers and lecturers. Listed categories of efficient evidence show clearly which kind of output is accepted: namely those listed in 'so called' collections of 'citation indexed' journals such as Thompson Reuters' ISI web of knowledge, Scopus and Springer Link. Archived items of audiovisual material including metadata and further supplementary descriptions are not to be found in these sources and it seem they will never be; neither will journals connected to this kind of 'rare disciplines' that use audiovisual materials and metadata. My paper focuses on ways of knowledge communication in this field and on some reasons of their actual status embedded into the competitive thinking of institutionalised higher education. What role can audiovisual archives with their collections play in this context? A vision can emerge from the findings, which should be brought into a discussion that reaches beyond archive and university walls.

Introduction

Academic research is probably one of the most rigorously and consistently evaluated sectors in modern society. To many of us working in the field of social sciences and humanities, bibliometric evaluation parameters for knowledge quality in the era of audiovisual collections and documentation can raise contradictory issue. Striving for the application of most advanced technologies in distributing knowledge and in its compaction, the omission of audiovisual documents that include processed knowledge in popular evaluation formats is an anachronism. This would be analogous to an imaginary

---

[14] First published: Jähnichen, Gisa (2012). Turning Audiovisual Archives into Scientific Assets. *Journal of Knowledge Management Practice, No.12/3*, 139–146.

world government dictating that fax machines have to replace email communication for the sake of fax machine producers. I am often surprised by editors who demand a limitation of audiovisual supplements although they might contain the main information of a scientific study. As in the very beginning of collecting audiovisual documents, pictures and sound are suspicious carriers of knowledge. They are considered to be less reliable owing to their primary characteristic depicting intangible contents that cannot be denoted in verbal expression thus being excluded from verbal discussion. Despite the fact that the linguocentric (Seeger 1977: 47) approach does not prevent manipulation and unreliability, we may ask if verbal discussion remains the only mean of scientific knowledge distribution. And will it be so forever in the future?

Going through an academic career means going through endless evaluation processes and – in some cases – finally ending up as an evaluator oneself. The whole complex process of knowledge accumulation will then be expressed in some remarks referring to regressively quantified percentage annotations, thus serving as rationale for decisions.

THE SITUATION OF HUMANITIES AND SOCIAL SCIENCES IN THE ERA OF IMPACT FACTOR AND CITATION INDEX

Some years ago, Richard Smith (2006), the editor-in-chief of the mighty British Medical Journal raised the question of flaws of peer review, the amateur quality of editors' work, the very concept of authorship and ethical issues such as corruption through funding and not publishing negative results. There can be added university practices of enforced joint authorship and abuse of power by supervisors and higher administration.

Can the social sciences and humanities be similarly vulnerable to destructive evaluation practices? Seemingly, the small economic impact of research in the social sciences and humanities as compared to that of research in the pharmaceutical or materials sciences could prevent corruption in big style, although we all may know single cases.

Blockmans (2007: 89-94) drafts a few important points that can be applied on the subject of evaluating academic research. Those who think that in the underestimated social sciences and humanities

"…methods valid to evaluate a variety of medical and natural science disciplines can simply be applied to other fields fails to recognize the specific research traditions and goals of other disciplines, particularly the humanities and social sciences. They are being measured according to standards that are unsuitable for their methodology and working practices. The reasons for this have been investigated by the Standing Committee for the Humanities of the European Science Foundation since 2000. The Arts and Humanities Citation Index (AHCI) of the ISI was judged to be unsuitable as an evaluation instrument for these disciplines and therefore should not be used by European policy-makers. Moreover, the AHCI is biased towards English language journals, it includes only a few of the best journals published outside of the U.S.A., and in no way takes into account the humanities' distinctive publication culture which revolves more around books and volumes. "

The ISI is focused on important articles in the first two years of their publication. In the humanities and social sciences generally, publications in any format remain relevant for decades (Peyraube, 2002: 14). Audiovisual material that is increasingly incorporated becomes even more valuable the longer it is preserved and equipped with updated metadata. It can – under certain circumstances – deliver reliable parameters for quality of academic research. In practice, I might not be the only one is surprised that some editors insist on reducing 'visual illustrations' or rejecting audio supplements for not being relevant, which should be translated as for not being in the scope of citation. Although over the years, archivists as well as media scientists have developed an effective and thoroughly tested system of audiovisual citation rules, the very character of audiovisual information seems to be the key problem in dealing with it in a conservative academic way that is based on linguocentric views.

If we try to search for journals on ethnology, musicology or ethnomusicology that are ennobled by the inclusion into a citation index such as Thomson Reuters we will find exactly one journal per subject: the Asian Ethnology, edited at Nanzan University, Nagoya, Japan; the Journal of Musicology, University of California Press, Berkeley, USA; and the journal Ethnomusicology, Indiana University, Bloomington, USA.

Ranking by number of native speakers	Language	Number of speakers in Million	Number of journals considered in the AHCI
1	Chinese	1,205	4
2	Spanish	429	24
3	English	428	**957**
4	Hindi	260 (Kariboli only)	2
5	Arabic	221	0
6	Malay/Indonesian	260	0
7	Portuguese	205	1
8	Bengali	193	0
9	Russian	144	6
10-13	German/	112	118
	French/		94
	Japanese/		5
	Vietnamese		0

Table 1: Out Of 120.000 Journals All Over The World 1225 Are Listed In The Ahci.

None of them includes audiovisual examples or a rich multi-format display of visual documents. Although these journals are undoubtedly of high quality, they could never be taken as the only representative part of academic discussion among ethnomusicologists, ethnologists or musicologists, who accumulate their knowledge primarily in audiovisual archives, in local languages, proceedings of small scale conferences, monothematic books and volumes that often include audiovisual supplements.

	SCI 2004:	SoSCI 2004:	% of SoSCI items
Number of source journals	**5968**	**1712**	**22.3%**
unique journal-journal relations	1,038,268	96,207	8.5%
total 'citing'	25,798,965	2,909,219	
total 'cited'	20,909,401 (difference of **18%**)	1,453,397 (difference of **50%**)	
'within-journal citations'	2,016,500	137,269	6.8%

Table 2: Descriptive Statistics Of The Jcrs Of The Science Citation Index, The Social Science Citation Index (Leydesdorff, 2006).

The humanities and the social sciences have the duty to break through this procrustean evaluation system of impact and citation indexes, which follows purely quantitative parameters in terms of academic investments such as project funding and manpower related to its outcome presented in ISI recognised journals. This duty arises from the distinct role of these disciplines not only in the academic world but also in human society as a whole. Blockmans explains:

"Issues of consuming societal importance, such as health policy, ethical and legal matters, cultural identity, religious thought, cultural changes related to technologies and social mobility, the distribution of resources and wealth demands a mode of direct communication between the researchers and the various social stakeholders. Every society is entitled to a deep and thorough analysis of the way it functions and has the right to research-based information on this matter; and, in highly developed societies, decisions in all areas are based on academic research" (Blockmans 2007: 89-94). Novotny et al (2001) called this "socially robust knowledge".

The Role of Audiovisual Archives

Audiovisual archives can play an important role in changing the situation in the social sciences and the humanities. Confronted with the speedily increasing amount of digitally born audiovisual documents, such archives, as directly communicated and diversely distributed knowledge sources can contribute to answer a few very important questions such as:

How is knowledge processing incorporated into audiovisual documents including metadata delivery authorised and related to research evaluation practice? Since we know that access to audiovisual collections is the main aim of all archiving efforts, we should now go further to enhance its quality in terms of societal development which is in many cases connected to academic research as a basis for decisions. Looking into university realities of publication and teaching issues, audiovisual documents, to date, are still undifferentiated and summarized as "illustrations" or as "non-scientific output" or as "supplementary works". What about those who work with non-verbally communicable content such as musicologists, scholars in the field of performance studies, film sciences, theatre sciences and history of arts and oral history? The often lamented loss of languages and their implied structural knowledge is on the way to becoming reality through ignoring their non-written shape. Languages in their oral form, which depend on sound rather than on visual symbols, will have no chance to develop academic significance although they are of utmost importance to the society in which they are used. Between English and those languages is a broad field of academically marginalised languages (see table 1). Not only the academic world that communicates mostly in English but also most reviewers who gain their reputation through English linguocentric approaches reproduce the unequal development of academic languages and the unequal standard in knowledge contribution around the globe. Now is the time to classify audiovisual documents seriously from the perspective of academic research quality. Being aware of technical and logistic matters that can only be controlled and overseen by professionals in various archiving institutions and organisations, the responsibility for this complex of social effectiveness should lead to classified co-operation standards between contents specialists and those professionals (Nisonger 1992: x ; 2003: 5, 23).

mono-format development	multi-format development

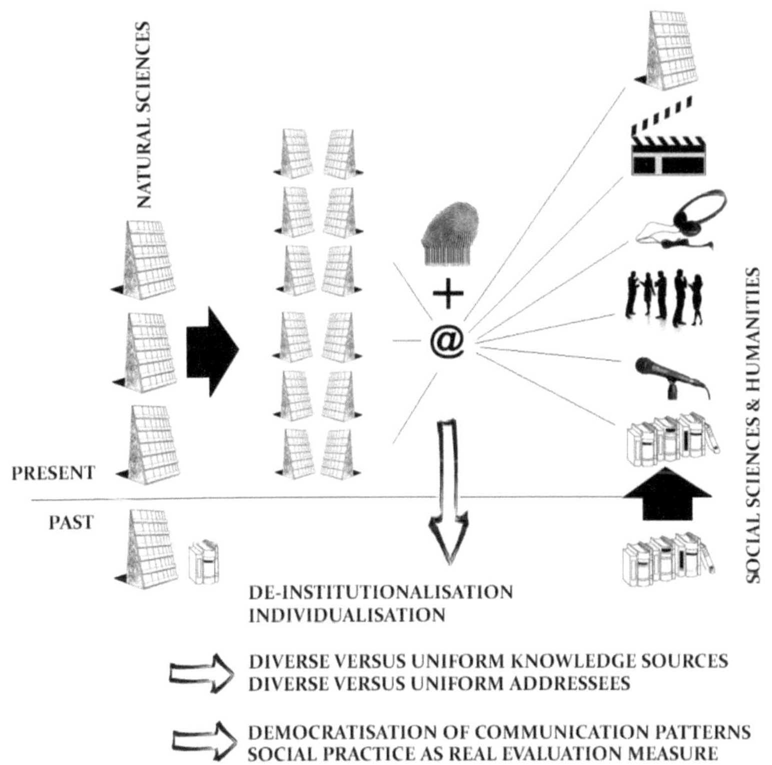

Figure 1: Knowledge distribution format from a historical perspective in natural sciences and in the social sciences and the humanities, partly caused through evaluation policies. Internet possibilities and digital identification tools can help to "Cross-Fertilize" knowledge distribution formats.

Do we need micro-institutional archives at universities and institutions of higher education and/or research which provide an authorisation as a standard requirement for the recognition of audiovisual documents including metadata delivery as scientific contribution? Seen from my experience, the answer can only be 'yes', we need them urgently, especially in countries with fast developing research sectors, where such micro-institutions do not as yet have any support from experienced archiving professionals. The main emphasis is not on national or even regional needs – advice and support is mostly of universal 'hard-science-like' nature, hence they can be provided from any part of the world. Rather, the crucial point is to establish micro-institutions at faculties or departments or at special sections, which have to be recognised as places of knowledge distribution with all necessary parameters of an archive in good standing quite similar to a standard publisher. Only then can audiovisual materials such as for example experimental compositions performed under special conditions, edited theatre discussions, fieldwork collections of various formats all coming with classified metadata, become an asset in terms of evaluable academic research contribution. And possibly only then can academia be compelled to use, distribute, and make accessible audiovisual documents thus enhancing in a broader sense its quality, which would help to include these knowledge sources into wide-scale research budgets.

The parallelism between recognition as equal part of academic evaluation and its treatment in social reality cannot be clearer than in the field of audiovisual archives. Even in highly developed countries, only a few archives could reach the status of being academically important thus socially relevant for policy makers, cultural decisions and economic strategies. The diversity of knowledge sources is deeply ignored in the academic evaluation industry where they are seen as distractions initiated by researchers in fields that have little "impact" on something of importance to the evaluation industry— their participation in the exercise of power through controlled knowledge distribution.

We could assume that such issues do not play any role in the era of the internet, but then, we overlook the fact that this very medium is itself ignored or at least downgraded due to its diversity in knowledge sources that are often incompatible with academic linguocentrism. This partly addresses the question of how future diversity in scientific communication will be treated in evaluation processes and how audiovisual archives in a large scale will respond to support knowledge distribution – for example through advisory help and backups to university micro-institutions which necessarily have to come into being for the sake of research in social sciences and humanities.

Finally, what can audiovisual archival organisations such as the International Sound and Audiovisual Archive Association (IASA) or others contribute to overcome procrustean evaluation standards in academic research that fail their main aims in many aspects, to serve the society through improving academic research quality?

The Archivist's Viewpoint

Schüller (2008; 10) describes in his inimitable style how among scholars of developing countries – he relates his observation to those from the former East European social system – there exists a "...significant distrust of any cooperative solution. Although researchers produced field recordings under the aegis of their employing institutions,..., they considered these recordings "their" property. This attitude, combined with a widespread habit in anthropological disciplines to claim sort of exclusive rights for certain research topics, regions, or ethnic groups, has even led to the foundation of parallel institutes under one parent institution's roof. A standard comment on the recommendation of cooperative models was often the assumption that such cooperation would only end up in the theft of one's own field documents by rivals from the same discipline. Fortunately, there are clear signs that with further societal development this attitude is fading out."

Additionally, Schüller (2010) remarks that audiovisual collections that represent an important part of scientific efforts in the field of social sciences and humanities were ignored over decades by scholars who could have been much better prepared for their own fieldwork through notice of previous recordings that are accessible in public archives. He criticizes these one-project-stand scholars for degrading archival values. His correct observation, however, seems to reflect the result of current academic evaluation practices that do not care about audiovisual sources and their exploration. Thus researchers are not encouraged to deal with "non-verbal" sources such as audio or video recordings in a comprehensive way. For their "market value" as researchers, the verbal discussion of written sources, illustrated with some specific experiences, is far more imperative. In a few cases, ethnomusicologists entered academic discussions through cross-references that are partly known to journal reviewers, so, researchers ensure sympathetic consideration to their publication proposals. The coincidence of paradigm shifts in ethnological and musicological research in the 1960s and 1970s seems not to be the main reason for neglecting publicly accessible audiovisual documents. It can be partly seen as an adaptation to academic quality standards as well as to competitive conditions at universities and research institutions in terms of a 'scientification' that abandons to a big part non-verbal knowledge. Thus, researching music 'without music' led in the following period to the retrospective impression of a factional struggle between those who are under the pressure of competitive 'scientification' and those who could still afford to deal with special details and to work in larger groups on selected areas.

A modern holistic approach to culture and society, in which, for example, ethnomusicology is extended to become a complex of interdisciplinary studies, needs both the exploration of existing and the production of new audiovisual documents. These interdisciplinary studies require pioneering in and with non-written sources (Edmondson 2004). But they are – unfortunately – often followed by 'source-biased' reviews for 'not citing professional literature'. Therefore, the introduction of audiovisual document "publishers" that are equally evaluated is absolutely essential to many subjects in social sciences and humanities.

Outlook or Publishing the "Unpublishable"

To turn audiovisual archives indeed into assets serving society in enhancing research quality and knowledge distribution, audiovisual archive organisations could help to develop models for these publisher-like micro-institutionalised archives in terms of audition and recommendation based on the rich experience of its members working in different sections and committees. The high reputation of the organisations' international body in collaboration with other national or local organisations dealing with audiovisual archiving can have an important effect on an urgently needed breakthrough in scientific evaluation practice, especially in fields where scientific linguocentrism meets intangible knowledge that unfolds in art production and their audio-visualised reflection. To connect competencies related to content and related to information technology, new conditions for co-operation in small scale archiving environments have to be negotiated in a way that evaluation parameters can be applied on both the content and the technological aspects. Therefore I call for practical solutions that can contribute to a multi-format recognition of knowledge assets.

References

Blockmans, W. (2007). *The underestimated humanities and social sciences*. The Authors Volume compilation. London: Portland Press, 89 – 94.

Edmondson, Ray (2004). *Audiovisual Archiving: Philosophy and Principles*. Paris: Unesco, Information Society Division.

Leydesdorff, L. (2006). *Mapping Interdisciplinarity at the Interfaces between the Science Citation Index and the Social Science Citation Index.* http://www.leydesdorff.net/sci_sosci/index.htm, last retrieved 2 October, 2010.

Nisonger, T. E. (1992). *Collection evaluation in academic libraries: a literature guide and annotated bibliography.* Englewood: Libraries Unlimited.

Nisonger, T. E. (2003). *Evaluation of library collections, access, and electronic resources: a literature guide and annotated bibliography.* Englewood: Libraries Unlimited.

Novotny, H., Scott, P., Gibbons, M. (2001). Re-Thinking Science: Knowledge and the Public in an Age of Uncertainty. Cambridge: Polity Press.

Peyraube, A. (2002). Project for Building a European Citation Index for the Humanities. Strasbourg ESF: Reflections, 14–15.

Schüller, D. (2008). *Audiovisual research collections and their preservation.* Amsterdam: European Commission on Preservation and Access.

Schüller, D. (2010). Discussion of the paper "Impact factor, citation index and other friendly fires in humanities: can audiovisual archives be turned into assets?" presented by the author at the *Annual Conference of IASA/AMIA* Philadelphia: Loews Hotel, 5 November 2010.

Smith, R. (2006). *The Trouble with Medical Journals.* London: RSM Press.

Seeger, Ch. (1977). *Studies in Musicology, 1935-1975.* Berkeley: University of California Press.

Audiovisual Documents as Ethnomusicological Sources in Southeast Asia[15]

Historical Conspectus

All around the world, archiving and documentation is a discipline of increasing importance for ethnomusicological studies. The possibility to record sound and movements and, thus, make the audible and visible part of any music culture reproducible, independently of time and space, led, to a great part, to the existence of ethnomusicology. Moreover, the very nature of sound and related movements as the main subjects in studies of performing arts needs to be imagined in a way that makes serious investigations provable. Thus, audiovisual documents are becoming intellectual assets of a comparable level to scientific discourses fixed on paper, preferably in journals represented in an international citation index. Nevertheless, the significance of audiovisual material is based on a special treatment that must develop the 'pure material' into a "document". I will come back to this question.

Most of the early audio and video material obtained by scholars from Europe and North America and stored as larger parts of anthropological collections turned out to be unassailable documents. A whole school of early ethnomusicologists, who were partly inspired by the systematic approaches of the Berlin School of Comparative Musicology—which, by the way, started with an analysis of the Thai Court Ensemble Repertoire—, explored Southeast Asian regions such as Indonesia with Jaap Kunst (1891–1960) and Mantle Hood (1918–2005), or Indochina and Myanmar with Jacques Brunet, Alain Danielou (1907-1994), who followed

---

[15] First published: Jähnichen, Gisa (2011). Audiovisual Documents as Ethnomusicological Sources in Southeast Asia. *Proceedings of the 2nd ICTM Study Group PASEA Symposium, Singapore, 2010*, 132-136.

59

partly the preceding ethnographers Gaston Knosp (1874–1942) and George de Gironcourt.

Southeast Asian music cultures contributed, from the very beginning of recorded sound, to the collections of museums and universities far away from their origin. If we have a short glance at the stock of primary recordings from Southeast Asia stored in the most popular museums, archives and libraries of the Western world, we can see that audiovisual documents deriving from Southeast Asian cultures have had an important impact on ethnomusicological methodology, especially on its systematic and analytical methods. These early developments were diluted with the upcoming "anthropological wing" of ethnomusicology, referring to Franz Boas (1858–1942), and finally led by Alan P.Merriam (1923–1980), extended and modified by John Blacking (1928–1990). Mervyn McLean comments on the period that followed this development:

> "When I tell people that in the past twenty years or so ethnomusicologists have largely given up field work, archiving, analysis, and comparison, they are apt to ask 'What's left?"(McLean, 2007, p. 133).

Although McLean is judging from the internal North American viewpoint and its supposed overview, the tendency to give up not only detailed fieldwork but to give up researching primary-experienced sound is remarkable. Often, article proposals by young, still idealistic scholars are currently refused by reviewers for being too analytical, too painstaking, and thus too boring and too complex due to its missing focus on one clear contextual issue.

The reason for this tendency is media-borne. With technological development and market expansion, paired with an increasing pressure on research institutions to publish and to innovate, a huge amount of audiovisual collections flooded the world of ethnomusicology. Only a very small part of it reaches the document quality of the early recordings.

Schüller, who was working on the TAPE project, remarks that he estimated the percentage of sub-optimally stored research collections to be 80%. This estimation is based on a fairly good personal overview of audiovisual collections worldwide (Schüller, 2008, p. 5). Schüller idealised institutional care from his perspective of identifying preservation—especially its technological and logistic aspects—as national responsibility. Although aware of quantities, he strongly underestimates private collections in their significance for research contents. Nevertheless, he creates visions—when innovatively translated—for any region of the world.

Meanwhile, a large amount of audiovisual recordings from Southeast Asia is travelling in the shape of digital files around the globe, leading a nomadic existence on many private computers. Only a small percentage of initially intended field recordings of the last few decades, made by researchers from the Southeast Asian region and from abroad, reached seriously working archives or at least some reliably working research institutions. The result is that young scholars often are left to choose audiovisual material from a wide range of volatile quality and equipped with doubtful descriptions to focus on one clear contextual issue. An even smaller percentage of these field recordings is accessible as archived items in the region itself. Thus, the world of audiovisual proof for ethnomusicological research in Southeast Asia becomes "really virtual" for those who are working in Southeast Asia. The sheer amount of recordings accessible through internet platforms seems to completely ignore the basic annotation work needed with sound and visual sources. Moreover, this situation is even worse because these recordings accessible through the internet sources are unelaborated and unannotated audiovisual recordings and are not yet "documents", which they may become through descriptive classifying, processing, preserving, and careful managing.

For many cultures of remote areas in Southeast Asia, where literature, music and dance are orally transmitted, institutions such as archives and media libraries are of utmost significance. They have to take on a guiding role, comparable to publishing houses in the world of print media, in close co-operation with researchers and networking institutions. As well as printed editions, audiovisual documents need to be updated and regularly re-collected. Therefore, they need to be supported in a qualified way by ethnomusicologists regardless of their institutional affiliation.

PRESENT-DAY REALITIES

One of the most disastrous observations I can make in Southeast Asia concerning audio and audiovisual documentation is the extreme lack of co-operation between institutions and individuals. For what reason does this exist?

Possibly, past colonial policies of dividing people into different groups deepened the pre-existing and further constructed social stratification. After the proclamation of independence, transformed or re-grouped hierarchies led to the continued existence of pragmatically organized collaboration of only short duration. Long-term inter-group solidarity, based on either utilitarian or altruistic reasoning, does not seem to be within the scope of any resource management.

Music and dance research suffers from this situation due to the dependence of these performing arts on audiovisual material and the subsequent transformation of the recordings into research documents.

Another problematic point is the fact that in most of the research institutions technical staff is administratively divided from academic faculty. Thus, joint tasks are often delegated to those who do not directly deal with content issues. Universities, colleges and other institutions of higher education or research are still well pampered with employees, and many researchers, postgraduates or project assistants regard archiving work as some kind of service provided by non-academic staff who just knows about technical details. This perception of technically demanding support can become very treacherous for researchers who really want to benefit from technology. To come with the first secret: it's not only a technology; it's a completely different scientific approach. While humanities in general, and the sciences on art and music in particular, were based on knowledge gained from written documents, in contrast, audiovisual technology enables one to trace back performances in their actual shape as primary sources. Therefore, joint efforts to overcome named problems are of utmost urgency.

A group of pioneers should come forth who are willing to take up the challenge and transform audiovisual material that is already collected into serious audiovisual documents, into scientific assets from which the whole region could benefit. One step is the formation of the Laón-Laón project[16] under the leadership of the University of The Philippines and supported by international archival organisations. Additionally, small-scale university archives should be established to convert private material into authorised and well cared for audiovisual documents. University researchers dealing with audiovisual material should agree to qualify themselves continuously to care about their own results from various projects and experiments.

EXAMPLES

I want to demonstrate a case from Indochina. In 1992, my first audiovisual recordings were made with a Hi8 video camera and a DAT recorder. I thought that taping as much as I can, and then making a list with time codes and contents, would be sufficient. I had the opportunity to record a so-called flute-singing of the Khmu people living in upland areas of Vietnam, Laos and China ("Khmu *peng pi*" or "*peng tot* Khmu") in Moc Chau on 22nd December 1992, at the border between Vietnam and Laos.

---

[16] The Laón-Laón project aims institutional networking, initiates collaborative projects, education about and with audiovisual material and addresses questions of ecology and advocacy in archiving. Its second forum outlined possible working schedules and introduces dialogue partners. It is supported by the University of the Philippines Center for Ethnomusicology and the Japan Foundation. See: Laón-Laón 2009: A Forum on Music Research Centers in Asia II. Paññāsāstra University of Cambodia, Phnom Penh 24-26 November 2009. Presentation materials.

This kind of music making is very rare and it is hard to find a Khmu who is able to perform it. The flute-song is an interlocking singing of certain pitches and continuing flute playing by one single musician (almost women; I've never seen men practicing). The inserted phrases are short excerpts from sayings. This music practice, performed by elder women, is addressed to children. When I heard the flute-song for the first time I thought that the sung pitches may be those pitches missed in the scale of the flute. I measured the instrument and I tried to imitate the melodic shape of the piece without much success. But, the flute could play all pitches, therefore, for me there was no reason to substitute single pitches by singing them. In a later analysis I discovered that one and the same flute could play different modes and that different pitches were filled with vocal inserts.[17]ii The recording got a place as a curiosity in my first large collection that I studiously archived in the Berlin Phonogramm-Archiv, where it lived untouched far from reality. Thoughtless, I forgot about it until a broadcast journalist asked me to prepare a programme on curiosities. It took a very long time to find another opportunity.

Ueay Phan, a Khmu woman from a village near Luang Prabang, who is famous for still being able to play "Tot Khmu", performed her example on 28th August 2000. It took only 8 years to regard a former common music practice of Khmu people as disappearing. Therefore, it was becoming rare to an extent that people who can perform this kind of music are called "famous".

It was not the piece of music itself that made me worry; it was the notion that this kind of neglectful blindness toward collecting music that could have an effect not only on one, but on many other cases. I believed that I was not the only person to record the Khmu-flute-singing, further I believed that time in this region passes so slowly that I would have plenty of opportunities to care about my collected items later. Even worse was the fact that I believed I recorded just an "item" of musical sound. In reality, it was a practice that was fast

---

[17] That was definitely the way of thinking I had as a clueless young scholar grown on the materialistic ground of systematic approaches.

64

changing, due to fast emerging economic turns that promoted technologies unknown to this area but without providing the possibilities of cultural balance. It should have been my duty to think ahead to the future of that music, as well as to contribute to such a balancing system. Since then, I have taken the transformation of any audiovisual material into audiovisual documents as seriously as the whole recording project itself.

Figure 1: Excerpt from a transcription of Khmu flute-singing made from the recording 601 of the Archives of Traditional Music in Laos. (Ueay Phan, Luang Prabang District, 2000).

CONSEQUENCES

To take further transformation of audiovisual material into audiovisual documents in Southeast Asia really seriously, a few preconditions have to be carefully planned:

An archive that stores primary recordings on any type of media, or as electronic files, cannot work as a restrictive institution in which the main focus is economic competition. If so, the stored "items" become an economic asset instead of a scientific asset. Unfortunately many colleagues still consider their recordings as economic assets rather than documents that have to be authorised and that have to be accessible to guarantee the possibility to trace resulting knowledge back to its sources. In print matters, no scientist would hold his writings hidden to the public for being afraid that other colleagues could rob his ideas. Scientific ideas are borne to be disseminated. Hence, articles and books have to be written to reach their destination, and audiovisual items have to be carefully edited as well, then they can be called "documents". At that point, they have the same strength of evidence as other scientific sources. All of this means that responsibilities have to be shared and networking is the only way to be successful in that field. Santos asks further:

> "If we are indeed interested to know of each other's cultures and the relationship of our own to these cultures, our research must take on a different direction. This is where collective research must be cultivated" (Santos, 2009, p. 10).

Until now, not a few researchers follow strictly their funded project direction, in which professional archiving is often not included. Networking between researchers of different institutions outside the financial safety of their projects rarely occurs. This condition must be changed. Throwing files, via Youtube or even more serious internet platforms, into the World Wide Web is not editing, it is simply a way of distributing material. First, all recordings need carefully reviewed metadata and cleared production modes. All these things need a high degree of professionalism, which unites technological and content-related knowledge.

As a final example, I would like to show you some recordings from Attapeu and Sekong, the poorest provinces in Laos. The villages, where the archive staff of the National Library to which I belonged as well, carried out so-called cross-sectional research projects, which were quite cut off from the rest of the country. Only in the dry

66

season, a dirt road connected the villages with the main road heading to the Mekong River. In the rainy season, the villages are connected to other villages through smaller water streams.

People here regard their cultural activities as very important due to the fact that they share the territory with many different people such as Alak, Nge, Oi, or Katu communities. They do not compete in terms of organizing festivals with performances evaluated by a jury. They just want to keep a few things in flow. They do not know how "famous" they will be in a couple of years. The cross-sectional recordings we made there have to be repeated in a sequence of 3 years. The recordings are publicly accessible in the National Library. The village gets copies of all recordings and photographs. Every time we come for a visit, we have a media-performance after the recording session. People discuss their contributions. They are aware of their value and they know, too, that the recordings are not "fixed items", but that the songs and other music can be played differently next time, and I think that is a very important and constructive result.

To develop a wide networking group of researchers—regardless of their institutional connection—we need everybody's innovative ideas and the deep insight that audiovisual material transformed into documents will be an indivisible part of our future working tools.

Although the flood of audiovisual recordings seems to overwhelm us, we should always be aware of the necessary quality, which needs as a precondition, a strong interrelation between technical implementation and cultural knowledge. Under these conditions, pure measurements and old-fashioned systematic comparison are not sufficient, although not out of date in general. This matter is really urgent due to the high speed of economic and social changes in Southeast Asian societies and their performing arts.

REFERENCES

Blacking, J. (1974). *How musical is man?* Seattle: University of Washington Press.

Danielou, A. (1957). *La Musique de Cambodge et du Laos.* Pondicherry: Publications de l'Institute Francais d'Indologie.

Edmondson, R. (2000). "Archiving 'Outside the Frame': Audiovisual Archiving in Southeast Asia and the Pacific," Film History, Vol. 12, No. 2, *Moving Image Archives: Past and Future* (2000). Bloomington: Indiana University Press, 148-155.

Gironcourt, G. de (1940). *La geographie musicale: valeur de la tradition musicale pour l'etude des races humaines devoir de sa preservation en Indochine.* Hanoi: Imprimerie Trung Bac Tan Van.

Gironcourt, G. de (1942). Recherches de Geographie Musicale en Indochine. *Bulletin de la Société des Etudes Indochinoise 7*, 1–174.

Hood, M. (1980). *Evolution of Javanese Gamelan.* Taschenbücher zur Musikwissenschaft [Pocketbooks of musicology]. 62. Wilhelmshaven: Heinrichshofen.

Jähnichen, G. (2009). The 'digital butterfly net' of ethnomusicologists and its impact on audiovisual archiving. *IASA Journal, 34*, December 2009, 83–90.

Knosp, G. (1912). *Rapport sur une Mission Officielle d'Etude Musical en Indochine.* Internationales Archiv für Ethnographie, 20.

Kunst, J. (1950/2nd ed., expanded, retitled Ethnomusicology, 1955; 3rd ed. 1959). *Musicologica: A Study of the Nature of Ethnomusicology, Its Problems, Methods, and Representative Personalities.* Amsterdam: Royal Tropical Institute.

Laón-Laón 2009: *A Forum on Music Research Centers in Asia II.* Paññāsāstra University of Cambodia, Phnom Penh. 24-26 November 2009. Presentation materials.

McLean, M. (2007). Turning Points: Has Ethnomusicology Lost its Way? *Yearbook for Traditional Music, 39,* 132–139

Merriam, A. P. (1964). *Anthropology of Music.* Evanston: Northwestern University Press.

Santos, R.P. (2009). The Relevance of Research and Cultural Preservation to Real Life. Laón-Laón 2009: *A Forum on Music Research Centers in Asia II.* Paññāsāstra University of Cambodia, Phnom Penh. 24-26 November 2009. Presentation materials, 8–13.

Schüller, Dietrich (2008). *Audiovisual research collections and their preservation.* Amsterdam: European Commission on Preservation and Access.

THE "DIGITAL BUTTERFLY NET" OF ETHNOMUSICOLOGISTS AND ITS IMPACT ON AUDIOVISUAL ARCHIVING[18]

The paper discusses the changing self-understanding of ethnomusicologists from enthusiasts pioneering in forgotten areas of the world to a species of networking researchers using all facilities of the World Wide Web and audiovisual databases. Aside from some unclear interpretations of user rights, there are important ethical challenges to observe, which are based on a fast re-positioning of humanities in the actual field of scientific efficiency. What will remain from the sublime discoverer's attitude and what will be the substance of another quality in ethnomusicological research? Talking about the "digital butterfly net" we should focus on what we call a "butterfly" and how it changes its shape, rather than re-examine its digital being. Finally we have to re-examine our supposedly universal parameters of "scientific efficiency" from different viewpoints, and we should become aware of prospective demands which need to be met by audiovisual archivists and ethnomusicologists in their socio-functional context.

INTRODUCTION

In the last decades, ethnomusicologists have continuously changed their aims regarding the material they gather for their own scientific purposes.[19] From today's point of view, it is hard to recall the

---

[18] First published: Jähnichen, Gisa (2009). The "Digital Butterfly Net" of Ethnomusicologists and its Impact on Audiovisual Archiving. *IASA Journal, 34*, 83-90.

[19] Some of them strongly assert their difference from comparative musicologists. This seems to be fully understandable insofar as comparative musicology is strongly identified with the early Berlin school. On the other hand – just discussing the method of comparison – this association between today's ethnomusicologists and comparative musicology, does not seem to be a necessary one. Fortunately, such aversions do not affect other fields of the humanities such as comparative

70

prevailing sound environment as well as the revolutionary changes regarding sound capture and conservation around a hundred years ago, when the only way to reproduce music was through a further live performance. The option of listening to music and sound from places outside the average living space of developed areas in Europe and Northern America seemed to be unaffordable. Thus the quite awful sound of a cylinder recording was the window to the unknown sound world, and was deemed worth keeping. Compared to first class live sound, the sound was a fascinating mystery. Thus field recordings inherited an aura, which came to take on a life of its own. In the very first days of field recorded sound, some musically interested people – not yet musicologists – recorded music just because the possibility existed. They carried equipment and material over long distances to challenge technology and to prove their ability to deal with it. The shape of that butterfly seemed to be determined by adventures that had to be survived getting to the field and getting back in 'civilization'.[20][76] Gouda describes the package coming with the aura:

Europeans have depicted native peoples as unruly children, for example, or as mystics who wallowed in a spiritual harmony with nature revealed in an existential freedom that most citizens of the modern Western world had long since lost. In this construction native people became idealized 'strangers in paradise', who lived their daily lives without conflicts and contradictions and were unhampered by private property or divisions of labor. (Gouda 2008: 119).

---

linguistics or comparative sciences of cultures. The method of comparison, which is always our independent presumption, between issues we already know and issues we learn later, cannot be blamed for limited world views and resulting wrong directions that emerged from a few ideas of the early Berlin school of Comparative Musicology. However, even those so-called wrong directions were not completely useless.

[20] As for example, Cecil Sharp, one of the first 'hunters' or his predecessor Francis James Child, who was robbing rather than hunting.

The recorded music and the performing people were more or less a confirmation of the geographic distance travelled and the apparent strangeness of their cultural expressions.

Today, while talking with sound engineers or technicians who sometimes accompany field excursions, a few of these attitudes can still be observed. However, real enthusiasts were growing in the shadow of the presumed business, who – although wrongly – aimed at a revived philosophy of musical universality through technological progress:

...it will not become so as long as our musical vision is limited to the output of 4 European countries between 1700 and 1900. The first step in the right direction is to view the music of all peoples and periods without prejudice of any kind, and to strive to put the world's known and available best music into circulation. (Grainger, Percy, broadcast over radio WEVD, New York, 20 June, 1933 – quoted according to Balough 1982: 113).

RANK GROWTH WITH PRINCIPLES

When sound recorded in the field became available via broadcasts and on records, the particular aura of field recordings was strongly kept alive, although more than a few recordings were done in well-equipped studios or under comfortable staged conditions all over the world.[21] The guild of early ethnomusicologists – who were not yet called as such, but were emerging in those years of technological news on account of their desire to organize their sublime studies even more effectively, or at least for their wish to ease hard field work consisting of long hours spent with the transcription diary on their knees in strange surroundings and under strange conditions –

---

[21] For example, Ellis and Hipkins, specialists on temperament and pitch of the Broadwood Piano Company, measured non-diatonic and so called non-harmonic tunings of Asian instruments that were brought to Europe. They studied Central Javanese music during a gamelan appearance at the London Aquarium 1882 and Chinese court music at the International Health Exhibition in 1884.

was initiated by ethnographers such as Jesse Walter Fewkes[22] or Béla Vikár,[23] described by Bartók as "the well-known man of letters and folklorist, who, without any musical knowledge, was the first to have recourse to a phonograph" (Bartók, Suchoff 1992: 60). Bartók learnt, possibly from Percy Grainger, the importance of the phonograph as a working tool in research. Far more influential on later ethnomusicological studies was the work of the Russian folklorist Evgeniya Lineva, who "was perhaps the first person ever to use the phonograph for field recordings, in 1897" (Bird 1999: 121), which is not true (since we know that Fewkes recorded in 1890), but nevertheless it seemed to be important in the competitive relationship among nations of that time. Unfortunately she started to de-personalize recordings through grouping of recordings and averaging out in simplified transcriptions. Hence she had a certain influence on creating musical nationalism, as seen in Stravinsky's compositions, which occasionally incorporate her "scientifically proven" folk chorus style as an indication of being truly Russian (Cross 2003: 16). Her documentation practice was widely adopted among East European ethnographers and later ethnomusicologists.

In Great Britain, as Bird describes in his Percy Grainger biography, the system of collecting was almost ideal, but it proved to be a source of argument in subsequent years between Grainger, Cecil Sharp and other members of the folk-song 'establishment'. Not only did it throw into bold relief a sharp divergence of attitude to the basic folk-song material, but it threatened to expose the frequently hitand-miss and sometimes dishonest techniques of other collectors. Grainger had little faith in the pencil-and-pad approximations of his contemporaries. (Bird 1999: 121f.).

---

[22] Fewkes made the first 'field recordings' in 1890 among the Passamaquoddy Indians of Maine. He tried to document the existing lifestyle and rituals of the Zuni and Hopi tribes, and made the first phonograph recordings of Zuni songs.

[23] The Hungarian Béla Vikár (1859–1945) began recording in the field in 1896

Despite the wide and wild collecting of whatever was accessible, the main purpose of collecting musical expressions as well as spoken folktales, poems or childrens' rhymes of that period was the "scientification" of musicology using the measuring tools of the so-called exact sciences.

Frequencies were one of the important areas of discussion. Nowadays some of the very early outcomes appear ridiculous as for example the insight of Ellis himself in co-operation with Alfred James Hipkins, who found that the prevalent notion that pentatonic scales had developed in Asian cultures because of insensitivity to the subtleties of the semitone: "It is found that intervals of three-quarters and five-quarters of a Tone, and even more, occur.

Hence the real division of the Octave in a pentatonic scale is very varied".[24] But it did not prevent later errors arising, for the earliest seem always to be the most enduring.

So, we still find similar expressions in many modern scientific works (Gramit 2002: 53; Jacksonand Pelkey 2005:145, 162).
As well as the first musicological insights, a major focus within the Berlin school, early records were made for eternity. The year of production was rarely printed on the record label. The belief that the transitoriness of music, dependent on real-time, could be captured on a wax cylinder or on a disc, resulted in the delusion that music could be captured and measured for eternity. Another misconception resulting from the aim of recording for eternity was that these captured musical expressions are fixed for ever and the material itself becomes eternal as well. From the viewpoint of audiovisual archivists who deal with early collections it can be said:

Both the collectors in the field and those whose sources were totally eclectic were intent on publishing the fruits of their work. It is therefore necessary to make a distinction between the means of collecting and between the kinds of song collections that were

---

[24] Journal of the Society of Arts, 1884, Oxford University. No page number.

published. It is also necessary to distinguish between the collecting of songs, by whatever means, and scholarship about collected songs. Although it may appear paradoxical, the first published collections of traditional songs were drawn from eclectic sources, and were followed later by the results of collecting in the field. The term 'song collections' is therefore used for an anthology of songs from various sources; and 'song collector' for a person who collects and edits such songs for publication. A compilation of songs gathered from 'live' informants and performers in the field is regarded as a volume of 'collected songs', and the gatherer and compiler of such a collection is referred to as a 'collector of songs'" (Shepherd 2003: 43).

Increasingly, the world of ethnomusicological research became a world of recorded material rather than of live music practice. Charles Seeger advised Sidney Robertson..."record everything! ...Don't select, don't omit, don't concentrate on any single style. We know so little! Record everything!" (Pescatello 1992: 141; also Baranovitch 1999: 159). Unfortunately, many recordings, which were completed in the trance of new technological possibilities, experienced not only a technical but also a descriptive abstraction. Questions like "do you have any Tasmania?", were standard.

Another observation is that collected material was more closely identified with the collector than with the collected subjects, hence it included not only the common abstraction according to regions but also the collector's conceptualisations, and it gained a life of its own. Thus the ethnomusicological butterflies already had to be taxidermically prepared, and this process was done by lower-level colleagues or enthusiastic students.

Early ethnomusicology, which is nowadays often interpreted as an extension of colonial intervention (Bohlman in New Grove 2005: Ethnomusicology, Post 1945 developments), was an eclectic and individualistic field of research, invented to prove emotional presumptions with evolving systematics, rather than a well-established scientific fundament of cultural colonialism, or, worse still, of cultural proselytizing. Personal interest, professional and cultural orientations crossed each other in a way that national or other lineages could be (and unfortunately were) constructed from various perspectives. The assumed knowledge was monopolized in private research archives or university libraries; the competition took place in written form. Through those discussions, rather than through real joint achievements of fieldwork and connected recording techniques, came a theory and subject of diverse arguments that followed diverse directions, as, for example, Jeff Titon seems to suggest, stemming from *the one and only*: "fieldwork relied on in-person observation and on data gathering through structured interviews, a method derived from the Trobriand Island practice of anthropologist Bronislaw Malinowski during World War I" (Titon 1997: 88).

At the same time, ethical considerations circulated, appealing to the researchers' responsibility:

In all cases, though, 'ethnography' denotes both intensive and extensive study of a human population. While it may involve formal or informal interviewing, it is distinct from journalism in that it is not "covering a story" but 'accounts for lives'. Ethnographers may focus, for example, on one class fraction or ethnic or racial population, one age group or one gender, but they do so within the context of overarching class and racial/ethnic formation, of the specificities of life course, of prevailing gender relations for that population. They may account for lives in the present, but they do so (or at least good ethnographers do nowadays) in a larger historical context" (Leonardo 2006: 207; (see also Shelemay 1997: 189-204).

Developments from that practice existed namely in the approaches of Mantle Hood, Alan Merriam, John Blacking, Gerhard Kubik, Artur Simon and several others, who were pointing to ethnomusicology as a new science worth incorporating into university curricula. Thus the identity of ethnomusicology in the practices and products of its scholars and in its academic and pedagogical structures became increasingly canonized in the decades after World War II, while in the decades approaching the end of the 20th century disciplinary boundaries began to blur in new ways, especially in the 1990s, precisely at a historical moment in which ethnomusicology was enjoying its most influential presence among the humanities and social sciences" (Bohlman ibid.).

This recognition had effects on recording institutions and on the recorded subjects themselves, as Aubert and Ribeiro describe:

Some specialist publishers dedicate themselves to this domain with expertise and discernment;[25] others, mostly concerned with the mass market, make occasional incursions according to the economic potential that such-and-such a fashionable genre

or famous artist represents. But these are rare exceptions, and most recordings only have an insignificant financial impact on the market, and therefore on the owners; or rather the performers of the genres in question. It is always useful to proclaim that a part of the royalties and other profits from such-and-such a disc has been given to the community of origin, and that a copy of the recording has been scrupulously restored to them or, if they do not have the means to use it, that it has been transferred to a local expert or representative institution" (Aubert and Ribeiro 2007: 66-67).

Here, the impact on audiovisual archiving becomes clearly evident. The scientific by-product is recorded sound and/or moving images, which make audible and which visualize the past of something that the common ethnomusicologist as well as the common ethnographer tries to understand. This "something" is the aim – the audiovisual outcome serves that aim, but it is not the aim itself. Although Aubert and Ribeiro describe an average case, the real practice seems to apply also to those audiovisual recordings, which were used for research far from their place of creation. Most of these recordings – whatever adventures were connected to their making – are entombed in audiovisual archives of the world with the same gesture of futility for inheriting scholars and their small community.

---

[25] For example Nonesuch records, Ocora, Pan-Records, and others (Post 2004).

As foreseen by Bohlman (2005) and several other ethnomusico-logists, the 'ethno' in ethnomusicology became inconsistent itself due to the enormous growth of technology and migration dynamics which did not only involve living space, but, more importantly, social changes and re-definitions of socio-cultural identities. The discussion about authenticity is becoming ludicrous. Order and distinctiveness are questioned. How can musical expressions as products characterise cultural affiliations in today's world? How representative of diversity in human life is the recorded manifestation? It seems that the more boundaries blur, the more categories rigidify in ethnomusicological discussions. [26] Ethnic pigeonholes still play a central role in many respects and recorded audiovisual material provides evidence even to sometimes contradictory interpretations. Again the material does not represent the recorded subjects, but rather the strength of evidence according to the researcher's opinion. Blacking once said about Grainger's visions:

The widely used label of 'ethnic' music implicitly denies the existence of the individual creative impulse, which has enabled people throughout history and in all parts of the world to produce infinite varieties of beautiful music. Percy Grainger hoped that knowledge and appreciation of this variety would become commonplace, so that music might become a universal language (Blacking 1989: 2).

Bearing in mind the actual situation, individualising – or re-individualising in view of early instances of recorded sound – instead of universalising musical language could be a step worth considering.

So, let us accept that butterflies can mutate individually. How does it affect audiovisual archiving?

---

[26] Discussions on cultural 'ownership' of genres, musical instruments, even single songs or pieces, especially as a discursive tool of post-socialist foundations of nationhood.

In the era of growing internet facilities, the average ethnomusicologist, and especially the student ethnomusicologist, finds the most
interesting mutations on the internet; the recording quality may be
poor but the metadata that can divulge the whole recording,
description, storage and access environment of a single recorded
item. Networking groups of students can reach all corners of the
world and find out where the best ukulele players or *belian*[27] singers
are concentrated, which repertoire they play or sing, how often, with
which cultural ideology they sympathise, and other less important
matters – parts coming together in a completely different butterfly
model. Observing this community of modernised researchers,
Malinowski might well cry in his diary of structured interviews.

The role of audiovisual archivists, finally, is to provide the wild
horde of a new ethnomusicological generation with sound and
moving images of respectable recording quality. The more
knowledge of environmental and technical details is shared in a
welcome democratic way via the internet, the more sophisticated
become qualitative demands. Archivists turn into networking
networkers and have to manage a huge amount of (more or less
competent) requests. Nowadays, everybody seems to have become a
little ethnomusicologist.

In the past, access was controlled through "hardware" institutions.
Now, access is controlled through a barely comprehensible software
market. Collected sound is ordinarily distributed outside of
institutions, and cannot be classified or peer reviewed. The amount
of possible subjects to be studied is countless. Thus institutionalised
audiovisual recordings take on a new function in guiding interests,
and promoting – finally – the recorded subjects. For researchers are
no longer limited by territorial access, unaffordable recording
equipment or travel difficulties, and their aim is changing
accordingly. They get away from monopolised knowledge areas of
schools and lineages and come closer to the very practice they were
claiming as their primary subject: the musical life of people in its
vast diversity, embedded into a thoroughly-investigated context of

---

[27] A kind of chant of the Kenyah people on Borneo.

time and space, slowly leaving the cultural circle of ethnic determination and encountering a more holistic view of the music's real environment, not only with regard to actual music practice, but also considering historical reviews and individual fates. This process is no less contradictory, as Aubert and Ribeiro comment:

The music genres of the world have certainly acquired merchant values; but they remain above all human values, in the noblest sense of the term. Their appearance in our immediate environment returns to us today an echo of society we live in: a society in crisis, questioning its foundations due to the recent eruption of plurality, but especially a society in mutation… (Aubert and Ribeiro 2007: 67-68).

CONCLUSION

Thus audiovisual archivists have to move on to become qualified guides and promoters. Although they always act as individuals, they are called on to respect the whole scientific background. That means the end of generalisation and the end of those once-so-comfortable universal audiovisual archivists who just had to consider all rules of TC-03 and TC-04 and did not need any further updates. The audiovisual archivist, still maintaining the best quality of audiovisual sources, becomes the most important controlling factor due to their competence. S/he should be the butterfly net him/herself. Therefore we urgently need to encourage archiving ethnomusicologists and ethnomusicological archivists to create a new species: the "sound environmentalist".

REFERENCES

Aubert, Laurent and Carla Ribeiro (2007). *The music of the other: new challenges for ethnomusicology in a global age*. Farnham: Ashgate Publishing.

Balough, Teresa (1982). *A Musical Genius from Australia. Selected Writings by and about Percy Grainger*. Music Monographs, 4. Nedlands, University of Western Australia Press.

Baranovtich, Nimrod (1999). Anthropology and Musicology: Seeger's Writings from 1933 to 1953. *Understanding Charles Seeger, pioneer in American musicology*. Urbana and Chicago: University of Illinois Press: 150-171.

Bartók, Béla, Benjamin Suchoff (1992). *Béla Bartók Essays*. Lincoln: University of Nebraska Press.

Barz, Gregory F. and Timothy J. Cooley, eds. (1997). *Shadows in the Field: New Perspectives for Fieldwork in Ethnomusicology*. New York: Oxford University Press.

Beck, Guy L., ed. (2006). *Sacred sound: experiencing music in world religions*. Waterloo: Wilfrid Laurier University Press.

Blacking, John (1989). *'A Commonsense View of All Music': Reflections on Percy Grainger's Contribution to Ethnomusicology and Music Education*. Reprint from Cambridge University Press Archive.

Bohlman, Philipp V. (2005) "Ethnomusicology. Post 1945 developments". *New Grove Dictionary of Music and Musicians*. Online edition.

Child, Francis James, ed. (1962 [1882-98]). *The English and Scottish Popular Ballads. 5 volumes*. New York: Cooper Square.

Gouda, Frances (2008). *Dutch Culture Overseas: Colonial Practice in the Netherlands Indies 1900 – 1942*. London: Equinox Publishing.

Gramit, David (2002). *Cultivating music: the aspirations, interests, and limits of German musical culture, 1770-1848*. Los Angeles: University of California Press.

Jackson, Jeffrey H. and Stanley C. Pelkey (2005). *Music and history: bridging the disciplines*. Jackson: University Press of Mississippi.

Leonardo, Micaela di (2006). Mixed and Riforous Cultural Studies
    Methodology – an Oxymoron? *Questions of Method in
    Cultural Studies.* Edited by Mimi White and James Schwoch.
    Oxford: Blackwell Publishing, 205-220.

Pescatello, Ann M. (1992). *Charles Seeger: A Life in American
    Music.* Pittsburgh: University of Pittsburgh Press.

Post, Jennifer C. (2004). *Ethnomusicology: a guide to research.* New
    York: Routledge.

Sharp, Cecil J. (1905). *Folk Songs from Somerset.* 2nd edition.
    London: Simpkin, Marshall, Hamilton, Kent.

Sharp, Cecil J. (1960 [1924]). *English Folksongs from the Southern
    Appalachians.* London: Oxford University Press.

Shelemay, Kai Kaufman (1997). The Ethnomusicologist,
    Ethnographic Method, and the Transmission of Tradition.
    *Shadows in the Field: New Perspectives for Fieldwork in
    Ethnomusicology.* Edited by Gregory F. Barz and Timothy J.
    Cooley. New York: Oxford University Press: 189-204.

Shepherd, John (2003). *Continuum encyclopedia of popular music of
    the world.* London: Continuum International Publishing
    Group.

Titon, Jeff Todd (1997). Knowing fieldwork. *Shadows in the Field:
    New Perspectives for Fieldwork in Ethnomusicology.* Edited
    by Gregory F. Barz and Timothy J. Cooley. New York,
    Oxford University Press: 87-100.

Williams, Sean (2006). *Buddhism and Music,* 169-189.

Yung, Bell and Helen Rees, eds. (1999). *Understanding Charles
    Seeger, pioneer in American musicology.* Urbana and Chicago:
    University of Illinois Press.

MULTIPLE ROLES OF A SMALL-SCALE ARCHIVE IN INDOCHINA[28]

The Archives of Traditional Music in Laos (ATML) was founded in 1999 by the Ministry of Information in co-operation with the Culture of the Lao PDR and the German Association for Technical Co-operation (GTZ). Eight years after zero, I look at the development of the Archives of Traditional Music in Laos, which is a media section of the National Library in the capital Vientiane. Special focus is given to the different roles of the archive, which are constantly changing. The profile of training and education with regard to media and music in the country is changing as well. These shifting situations brought about a new social consciousness of audiovisual archiving.

The ATML is a telling example of AV archiving in a low budget environment. This example should encourage other small scale archives in the world under similar conditions to find a productive and a progressive way for their future.

INTRODUCTION

When I first heard that I was to establish an audiovisual archive of traditional music in Laos, which was organised by the University of Applied Science in Emden, Germany, I was excited and started to imagine what could be done - but there were many fears as well. As I learned through my experience in Vietnam, I had to pre-empt unforeseen difficulties that seem typical of all assistance efforts in the region, but which I didn't want to experience in Laos again. For example, the lack of inter-institutional co-operation, restrictions on recording material from one jurisdiction to another, supply problems,

---

[28] Jähnichen, Gisa (2008). Multiple Roles of a Small-Scale Archive in Indochina. *IASA Journal, 31*, 62-69.

and time-consuming financial proceedings and so-called commercial resources.

In Laos, I experienced the following: although I had to carry out project work I could not take decisions on things such as acquiring archiving equipment, audio and video equipment - that was the task of the German management; I had to train the staff but I could not take decisions on training contracts or recruitment conditions - that was the task of the institution in Laos and the German management; I had to do research on acquiring new material but I could not decide how much time should be spent to get the material – that depended on other factors.

I had no choice but to trust that everything would be solved within two years. It might seem that I was in an awful situation, but I wasn't. In fact it was the same everywhere else. Even in Germany, as a Professor at the University, I cannot take decisions other than for myself. So I didn't have to change my personal attitude to work. Perhaps this was the most productive condition for me, because it forced me - and the staff - to press on and make sure that all would end well.

SOME COMMENTS ON MOTIVATION

The common European thinking about projects such as this - looking from a remote perspective without deeper insights - is that the most problems are of technical nature. Good quality equipment, enough money to undertake field recordings and safe storage facilities will achieve the desired results automatically. I learned that in principle it isn't wrong to think like that, but it is wrong enough to put an end to significantly archiving.

Being involved in a project such as this to establish archives in a so-called "underdeveloped" country it is easy to feel like "little princes from a rich star". It needs time to understand that one is not a prince and that the star is the same world and is not rich. In Laos, however, I never felt advantaged, but rather like somebody who needs help.

I think the first realisation that is needed to create useful and productive archives is a deep understanding of the sense of archiving. Therefore the most important initiative should be to persuade people to share this challenge, to be creative in linking individual knowledge of different cultures from the past with the present needs for a better future. We have to understand the word "better" in this context.

We need to know how to persuade people to be good co-workers, but also to get involved in what we are doing.

All the other issues about technical equipment, training and storage standards depend on this philosophy. The most unsatisfactory situation is a technically perfcct audio archive with staff and official visitors who are not interested in archiving and who treat the material with no respect.

Let me take you on a very short virtual tour through the development of the archiving context in which we were and still are working:

STORING

First of all there was no doubt that all the wonderful recordings and additions had to be stored safely. Initially the term "safe" did not mean the stored material but the safety of the property. Nobody should get access to the buried treasure of tapes and documents. It took more than a year to make it clear that safety of all the recorded material, including the sound and video information on the carriers, was the first priority, and including data integrity and regular inspection of the physical carriers.

It was urgent to bring the message home. Traditionally written literature on palm leaves can be restored hundreds of years later, and is very different from the comparatively very young recordings. If a palm leaf manuscript is stolen, not much is lost in terms of value. But when a sound recording on a digital audio tape is stolen, something must be done to prevent deterioration and to invest in the playback equipment. Seen through the eyes of audiovisual archivists, many of our administration teams did not understand this.

We slowly turned the safety issues round in a useful direction, especially with the help of our colleagues from the film and video institute, which is a member institute of the SEAPAVAA.

So, we started to be known as a department which stores very special material.

AUTHORISING

The second step was to convince musicians and collectors of the necessary documentation and descriptions of their collections and recordings. Undocumented and publicly inaccessible recordings and documents have no value to future cultural developments, including individual representation. Any single musician cannot testify to his authorship without an entry in an official archive. The notion of "you give to get it" needed time to be implemented. Thanks to national workshops and meetings, and thanks to a consequent policy concerning intellectual properties - even if not really successful in terms of national economy - we could accomplish a better understanding among our partners.

This success solved another problem, too: After Laos opened its doors to mass tourism many amateur ethnographers were active in the region. They recorded traditional music and dance and avoided official registration by underhand payment to the musicians and dancers. When the Lao staff would request recordings afterwards, it was very difficult to record musicians for less than the last payment. However, the main problem was that the musicians were not interested in playing for their own poor communities any more. A thorough study of those appearances resulted in the conviction that only officially registered recordings would protect the rights of the authors and that this value was higher than a single payment.

MEMORISING

Finally all the data entries, especially video material, serve as a memory of the communities. Most of the visitors from remote areas are searching for pictures and video recordings of technological interest.

Figure 1: Documentation on khen construction and use in the Lao language, edited with the help of the ATML, which visited and invited all khen players to exchange their experiences As an example of mouth organ construction, we selected two different types for illustration.

After watching video material, some of the workshops resumed their work. Now new mouth organ workshops exist in Xiengkhuang, Huaphan and Bolikhamsay areas where this kind of mouth organ is played by the Lao. Transfer of knowledge through audiovisual material replaces direct learning from living teachers and craftsmen. In an orally conditioned learning context of this society it seems to be easier to learn in this way than in highly developed cultures of writings and abstract codifications.

EDUCATING - ACTIVATING - MOTIVATING

The next step was the general change of the archive's role as a place for educating, activating and motivating culturally working people.

At the last ICTM conference in Vienna, I was able to present some of the surprising results in the development of dance traditions, which are of great national and religious significance. Without the activities of the few archivists in the ATML these achievements could not have been realised.

Figure 2: The National School for Music and Dance in Vientiane is working with additional teaching material from the ATML

CHANGING VIEWS - AWAKING PUBLIC CONSCIENCE

Thanks to international interest and the growing internal acceptance of audiovisual documents as knowledge transfer tools, the work of the archive changed the views of the public administrators on their cultural outcomes, their history, their current situation concerning their social and ethnic values. There is not one meeting or festival without recalling important events, which the organisers observed indirectly through our audiovisual documents. The archive is frequently asked for support of different ministries and institutions, and it is creating a kind of public conscience which cannot be avoided any more.

CREATING RESOURCES - RECOVERING KNOWLEDGE

Finally, after seven years, the archive found its place in the cultural and political landscape, and established a place for creating resources and recovering knowledge. But we need to defend and develop it continually on a daily basis.

Figure 3: Presenting music and dance at the That Luang Festival 2004 according to recovered local traditions of various areas

We now have to focus our skills on digitisation and a new kind of public access through the intranet of the National Library. This technical development will surely create a new context and further the role of this small-scale, but big spirited, archive in the small country of Laos, to rise as an example in the region.

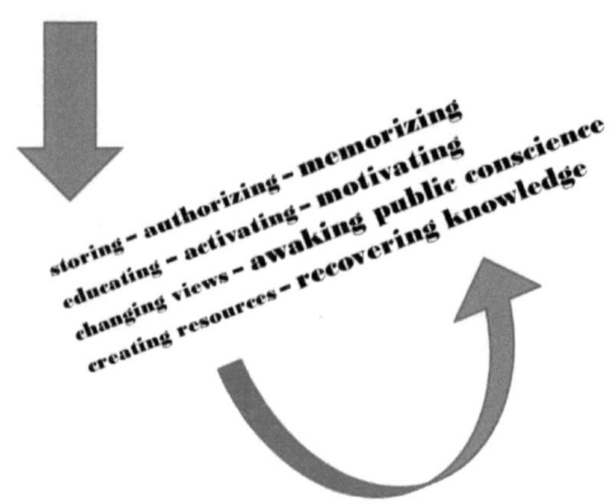

Figure 4: Contextual framework of the ATMl in Vientiane, Laos

REFERENCE: LITERATURE EDITED WITH THE HELP OF ATML, VIENTIANE:[29]

Jähnichen, Gisa: Re-Designing the Role of Phalak and Phalam in Modern Lao Ramayana. In: Wacana Seni, journal of Arts Discourse, ed. by Tan Sooi Beng, USM, Penang. (printing in progress, 19 p.). 2008.

Jähnichen, Gisa: Feldforschung in Theorie und Praxis: Das Archiv fUr Traditionelle Musik in Laos, in: Um - Feld - Forschung. Erfahrungen, Erlebnisse, Ergebnisse, ed. by Julia Ahamer and Gerda Lechleitner, Verlag der Osterreichischen Akakdemie der Wissenschaften, Wien 2007: 3 15-331.

Nattasin - Basic styles of Lao Dance, edited by Gisa jahnichen, National Library of Laos,Vientiane 2006 (144 p.) + CD-ROM-Edition, (special national edition)

Jähnichen, Gisa: Local Typology and Individuality of Hmong Song Melodies, in: Guandu Music Journal 4, edited by Schu Chi Lee,

---

[29] Content and format as being noted in 2008.

College of Music, Taipei National University of the Arts, june 2006: 161-212; ISSN 1814-1889.

Jähnichen, Gisa: Sardinian air in Lao pipes, in: Report on the Study Group Meeting "Folk Musical Instruments" in Vilnius ILatvia, April 2006, in: Tautosakos Darbai XXXII, ed. by Ruta Zarskiene, The Institute of Lithuanian Literature and Folklore, Vilnius 2006: 77-86; ISSN 1392-2831 .

Jähnichen, Gisa: Das Bengbong-Spiel der Brau in Laos: Soziale Ideen in instrumentalmusikalischer Praxis, in: Berichte aus dem ICTM-Nationalkomitee Deutschland, Bd. XIV/XV, ed. by Marianne Brocker, Bamberg: Universitatsbibliothek, 2005: 13-31; ISSN 0943-4224.

Jähnichen, Gisa: Pray woman and their musical duties, in: Shared Musics and Minority Identities -Papers from the third meeting of the "Music and Minorities" Study Group of the International Council for Traditional Music (ICTM), ed. by Naila Ceribasic and Erica Haskell, Institute of Ethnology and Folklore Research, Zagreb, 2004: 93-107; ISBN 953-6020-32-7.

Jähnichen, Gisa: Who are we? Cross-sectional preservation of musical traditions of ethnic minorities in its gender dimension, in: Report of the International Symposium on Preservation of the Arts Heritage of Chinese Ethnic Groups & Development of Contemporary Arts, Beijing: Chinese Academy of Arts, 85/230.

Kongdeuane Nettavong: Khen Ie siangkhen [Mouth organ construction mouth organ playing], edited by Gisa jahnichen, National Library of Laos, Vientiane 2002 (86 p.); (special national edition).

Jähnichen, Gisa: Manner weinen nicht, Manner sind nur komisch... – Wiegenlieder und die Vorurteile der weiblichen Zivilisation, in: Berichte aus dem ICTMNationalkomitee Deutschland, Bd. XII, ed. by Marianne Brocker, Bamberg: Universitatsbibliothek, 2002: 137-148; ISSN 0943-4224.

Jähnichen, Gisa: Laos: Traditional Music in Buddhist Context, CD-booklet, Tucson (Arizona): celestial-harmonies, 2-39.

Jähnichen (2002). The Archives of Traditional Music in Laos. 100th anniversary of the Berlin Phonogramm-Archiv. Ed. by Gabriele Berlin und Artur Simon. Berlin: Ethnologisches Museum, SMPK, 330-340.

Jähnichen, Gisa: Collecting principles and their obstacles - or: How to collect nothing, in: IASA journal, Nr. 18 (200 1), December, 15-22; ISSN 1021-562X.

Jähnichen, Gisa: Mundorgel-Akrobatik der Hmong in Xiengkhuang und Huaphan, Berichte aus dem ICTM-Nationalkomitee Deutschland, Bd. XI, ed. by Marianne Brocker, Bamberg: Universitatsbibliothek 200 I : 75-89; ISSN 0943-4224.

Jähnichen, Gisa: Research Report: Archives of Traditional Music in Laos, ed. by Gisa Jähnichen, Ministry of Information and Culture, National Library of Laos - FH Oldenburg-Ostfriesland-Wilhelmshaven,Vientiane 200 I.

Jähnichen, Gisa: Music from Laos, in: Buddha - transcending space & time, Sydney - Tucson (Arizona): celestial harmonies/ Art Gallery NSW, Ie 7869/14215-2, 18-20.

ACCESSING PEOPLE THROUGH ACCESSIBILITY OF AUDIOVISUAL DOCUMENTS[30]

INTRODUCTION

When I began working at the Humboldt University in Berlin, I had the rare opportunity to listen to one of the 'enfants terrible' of cultural studies, Prof. Mühlberg - one of the first professors to have been involved in the so-called 'future research' from the East at that time.

The opening remark in one of his lectures was a very simple question followed by an answer that marked a turn in my thinking. He asked us: 'Do you need a washing machine?' Everybody was sure: 'Yes I do, I need a washing machine'. His simple answer was: 'You do not need a washing machine - you need clean clothes!'

Now I ask you: 'Do you need access to audiovisual documents; do you need access to all the collections in the audiovisual archives?' Without a doubt, yes. With my new thinking hat on I would say: 'You need access to people!'

Audiovisual documents are part of our communication tools. They are part of our methods of structuring communication, which might be unintentional, but which aims to interact with others to create a better understanding of the audible and visible reality in different times and spaces. But, audiovisual documents are first of all not activities, even if they do represent activities and force us to act. Let us therefore focus on the main purpose of our work, while discussing the subject: Accessing People through Accessibility of Audiovisual Documents.

Unrestricted access to audiovisual documents can be one of the tools that have numerous possibilities. First of all, we should ask ourselves the following questions:

---

[30] First published: Jähnichen, Gisa (2006). Accessing People through Accessibility of AV Documents. *IASA Journal, 28,* 42-50.

If we have access to audiovisual documents, do we have access to 'reality'?

How do we deal with issues and activities of the past and how are they represented in audiovisual works?

Concerning our educational purpose we should also think about the following:

How well are we prepared in considering the being of audiovisual documents as a philosophical basis?

Finally, I will demonstrate the issue with two extremely different examples:

- People in remote areas of Indochina - their way of accessing the world and our way of getting access to them
- Students at German universities - already struggling with an overwhelming amount of audiovisual documents, but still hungry to know more.

The following scheme shows a few very basic ideas. Dealing with so-called 'audiovisual originals' in archives and museums, I and my colleagues often learned to interpret them as the 'original reality'.A few weeks ago a Malaysian teacher of the Academy of Arts took me by surprise when he asked me whether I needed an 'original copy' of a certain software program!

We can easily forget that we deal with copies of audible and/or visible events of the reality, not with reality itself, which always depends on space and time. So, we have a certain knowledge through our own physiological and psychological experience of reality, and we perceive the 'original' through the representing tool: the audiovisual document. This kind of knowledge helps us to compare realities with copies. Shortly after that useful first step into the world of audiovisual documents another awareness became evident: the transmitted knowledge of the technical copy of a visible and audible event of that reality.Transmission occurs through metadata, through subsequently shortened or abstract information; even conjectures about it. Owing to the character of the transmission, the comparability of authentic activities with technical copies is subject to our imagination and quite impossible. The more time has elapsed since the original event took place, the more we are dependent on the copies (recordings).

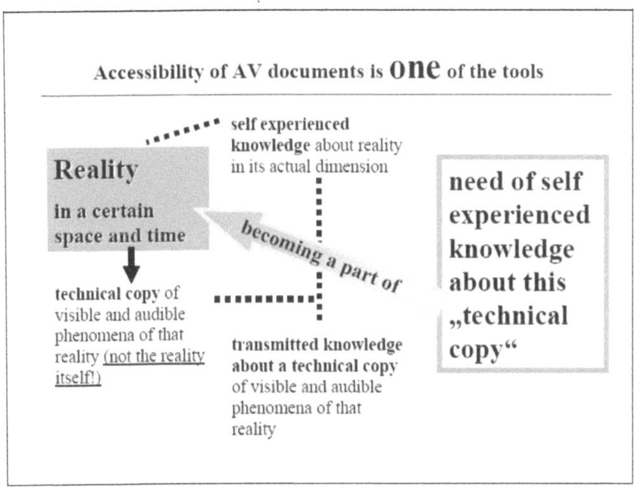

Figure 1: Consciously processing of "meta-realities".

And so the 'self-experience' through access to audiovisual documents becomes part of our 'meta-reality'.

Let us look at the second scheme: the relation between pink and grey shows the crossing of borders between 'real original' and 'real copy'. The borders between reality and its 'copy' can be wiped, and borders between the copy and the self-experienced knowledge of the copy can wiped too.

Another point of discussion is the ambivalent relationship between audiovisual information values as a tool of freely organised communication and as a marketable product. Both can be included in the same picture or sound; and it is primarily a question of the way we look at it and what we recognise.

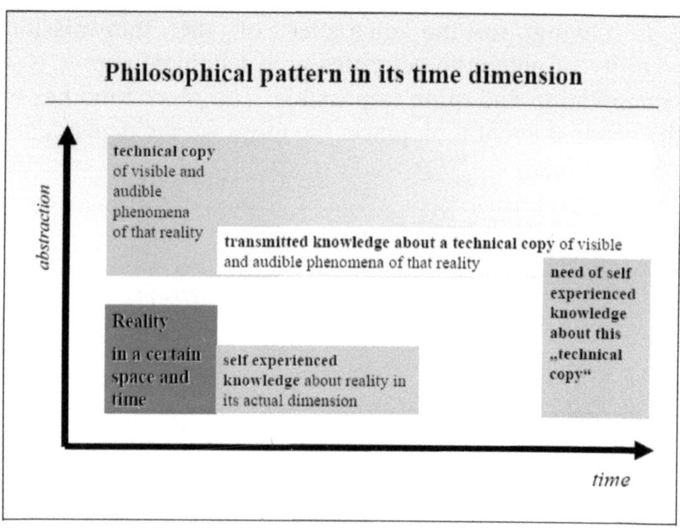

Figure 2: Reception of abstraction level in time correlation

These indistinct phenomena of the ultimate being of audiovisual documents lead us to a further important observation. We need an answer to the question whether audiovisual documents refer more to form than content, or - and this solution seems to be more practicable - whether the special being of audiovisual documents is reprocessing the original and is always created outside the material definition itself. So, what does an audiovisual document mean to us?

With regard to its form we can count on the realisation quality, the actual carrier format and the format of audiovisual availability; with regard to its content we should think firstly about its individual importance, and then about its economic, social, and cultural importance.

The latter are mostly declared by an abstract identity holder as an ethnicity, a village, a district etc, for the reason that all kinds of importance are to a certain degree born individually. So, the ambivalent behaviour of audiovisual documents continues in the level of social determination as form and content, as a thing and an' act, as things in action and as a reflection of things.

Finally we may surmise that we can define audiovisual documents, which include all these phenomena, only functionally for being a non-material bundle of meanings.

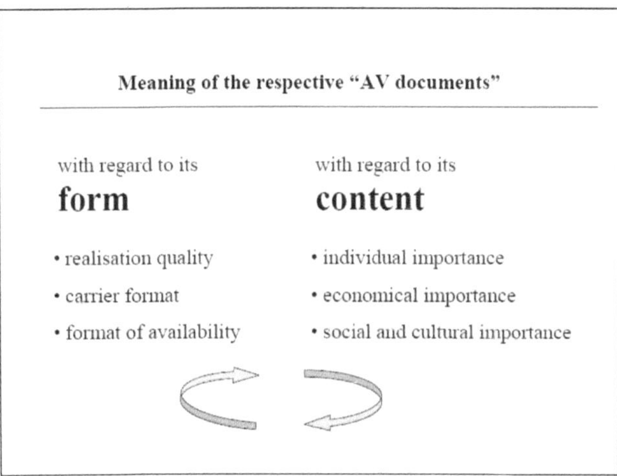

Figure 3: Form - content correlation as parameters of importance

Let us go back to the accessibility of this non-material bundle of meanings and ask: How does accessibility of audiovisual documents change our social behaviour?

At best, for example in the WITNESS Media Archive, accessibility is the key function of all subsequent actions, which can change lives for a better future:

'WITNESS is predicated on a strong belief in the power of video as a tool for change. In our work with our partners we have demonstrated how visual evidence can promote or be a catalyst of change when other audiovisual venues have failed, or proved less effective. The increasing audiovisual availability of video production and distribution tools provides a tremendous opportunity to expand the reach of media to some of the world's un- and underrepresented peoples.'[31]

In the worst case scenario, for example observing the discussion between students of the Johann Wolfgang Goethe University Frankfurt a.M. during a the seminar on Audiovisual Archiving in Musicology and Media Science during the 2006 summer term, we can find some of the answers, which were not dominant but evident in an alarming fashion. Those very students of the university demonstrated nearly every day against the general charging of tuition fees.

(a) If everybody could access all the relevant audiovisual documents and we could control all the collections that are published, journalists and scientists would be fully responsible for what they publish.

(b) On the other hand, we might not be interested in their publications anymore; and we would never have the freedom to prove their outcomes.

(c) 'No access' rates audiovisual documents more important to people who do not know - access destroys their fantasy.

(d) We are satisfied with information; we are very tired of proving facts.[32]

So, on the one hand we see a philosophical logic in the need for accessibility of audiovisual documents as a proven tool for accessing people, for letting them take part in the world of information, knowledge and art - on the other hand we see a oversaturated community among young intellectuals owing to disappointment and disillusionment in their daily life.

---

[31] Lile, Grace, Archives and Advocacy: The WITNESS Media Archive and Global Human Rights. In: IASA Journal No.26, December 2005: 30

[32] Students of the Johann Wolfgang Goethe University Frankfurt a.M. in the E-forum of the seminar in „AV Archiving in Musicology and Media Science", summer term 2006.

However, we cannot blame them for it. It is their reality. Let me show you two very different examples concerning the topic 'accessing people'. Both are relevant to the global context and both follow a certain pattern of civilized communication.

'Civilize' in terms of food means:

i) to eat or not to eat;
ii) more or less to eat;
iii) to eat a certain quality of food;
iv) to eat in certain surroundings; and finally again
v) to eat or not to eat.

All these sections can be recognized in audiovisual documents as well.

My first example leads us into the Sekong basin, a part of the Mekong system in Laos. The results of a very well organised field trip by the 'Archives of Traditional Music' in 2001 were excellent. We recorded eight hours of music on DAT, five hours of video on DVD, and took 144 photographs. The team noted every detail.

Figure 4a and 4b: Alak and Nghe people of the Sekong basin. (Photo: Gisa Jahnichen, March 2001).

We found and recorded musical examples from 12 different minorities of the south. The most obvious cultural changes occurred between two minority groups, the Taoi and the Alak, after resettlement in another location. Our aim was to record the music tradition; to get into contact with their communities; to build a first line of communication rather than a network; and to concentrate more on their cultural being, their musical and dance qualities, their interests. Did we only 'reach' them, or did we 'access' them?

Back in the city we decided to create a promotional video of brief cuts with incomplete sections of performances to gain real access to the people, not only in the desired area of the Sekong basin, but also to people who do not know about them. Now, three years after regular distribution of the video (content!) the amount of external, interested researchers and artists is growing and we hope that the people of the Sekong basin are not only reached by them . The following rough field report shows some issues that we had to face and analyse I order to achieve our goals.

REPORT

On the 2Sth of March 200 I at 6.00h we started our trip to the south. With one stop in Pakkading and one in Seno we reached Khongsedon at 18.00h.There we met Mr. Sisuk (DAFO) who gave us some information about the present situation in the province of Salavan.We found accommodation in the district guesthouse for one night. On the 26th we visited the Cultural Office of Khongsedon and left at 8:30h for Salavan which we reached at 10:30. We met Mr. Khamphui, the head of the Department of Information and Culture, and Mr. Bunthon, who became our local advisor for the next 3 days in the province of Salavan.After lunch we left Salavan for Tumlan which we reached at 14.45h.There we waited until 16.00h for the reception by the Cultural Office.Then we were introduced to Mr. Somlet, who was the local advisor for the Tumlan District. With him we went to Ban Dindak where we recorded 2 singers of the Katang (Bru)-Minority. After that we moved to Ban Phuthai, the neighboring village. In the house of an instrument maker we recorded 6 musicians, who played the khen, the so-i and the kachappi. There was no electricity and the whole village surrounded the house, where we recorded on the veranda in the light of a few candles. At the end we bought one of the instrument maker's khen and returned to Tumlan at 21 .00h. We found accommodation on the veranda of a newly built house of the district.

In the morning of the 27th we recorded a khen player and a female singer of the Katang-Minority in this house. Then we left for Salavan, which we reached at lunchtime. We took a shower in the bathroom of a restaurant and continued our trip to Samuai. The road was in very bad condition, so the trip of 139 km took about 7 hrs. We stayed in the house of Mr. Thuma who was a member of the Cultural Office of SamuaL We made an appointment with the musicians of the Kado-Minority. Next morning we vistied the Cultural Office and invited the musicians to the house of Mr.Thuma, where we recorded the S musicians on the veranda. The recordings took more than 4 hrs. After lunch we left Samuai for Muong Taoi which we reached at IS.OOh. There we recorded 4 musicians of the Taoi-Minority, who accompanied a singer on a drum, a rattle made from a beer can, a kachappi from the Salavan Lao people. Mr. Bunthon told us that the singer was the only in this district, so we decided to return to Salavan, which we reached at 19.30h.Wc stayed in a small guesthouse for one night.

In the morning of the 28th we visited the Department of Information and Culture and reported about our work in the districts of Tumlan, Samuai and Muong Taoi After that we went together with 4 musicians and one female singer to the house of Mr. Bunta. He was a first class musician as well as a traditional doctor. We recorded the ensemble, which included different sized khens, the drum, the sing. the buffalo horn clapper, the so-i made in the Chinese manner, one traditional and one modernized kachappi until 12.4Sh.After that we went to Pakse which we reached at 14.30h.We spoke to Mr. Sipaseuth in the Department of Information and Culture about our work and we arranged a later part of our trip with Mr. Uthay in the district of Pakxong after our return from Attapeu.

In the afternoon we checked the car, which was necessary after driving on the interesting roads of the Salavan province. We found accommodation in the house of Mr. Bouaket's relatives in Ban He. The next morning we recorded the famous singer of Ban He who was accompanied by a khen-player. Then we left Pakse for Attapeu.

We crossed the Boloven-Plateau. We reached Attapeu at 12.00h and searched for the head of the Department of Information and Culture.We found him in his house and he introduced us to the Mrs. Butsady and Mr.Yenkham, who became our local advisor in the province of Attapeu. In the afternoon we went with him to Ban Lanyao Tai. This village is of the Oi-Minority. There we recorded 3 musicians who played a set of Oi-khen, the bamboo toen and a bows harp.At 17.00h we returned to Attapeu. In the evening we were invited to Mrs. Butsady's house for dinner and a very good 'lauhai'.

On the 3Ist we went together to Phuvong. We had to cross the Sekong River by ferry. In Phuvong we found Mr. Khamson who works for the Cultural Office of Phuvong. He made an appointment with the musicians of the Brau Minority from the district for 14.00h. So we had time to go for a picnic to the riverside. But the road was so bad that we had to return. After lunch we waited for the musicians and dancers in the shadow of the veranda roof.

15.00h they started their performance with their ensemble of gongs that accompanied the dancers with their rice stamp sticks. Another piece was played with the gongs and S flat brass gongs followed by different dances and an epic song. The recordings were finished at 17.00h. We spent the evening together with Khamson's family and slept in their house as well. Next morning we recorded a few lullabies in Phuvong and two tube harpes, the gong ding and the ching ding. After that, we returned to Attapeu crossing the Sekong River where we waited nearly 2 hrs for the ferry. In the afternoon we were invited into the house of Mr. Khampon. We reported about our work in Ban Lanyao Tai and in Phuvong. We stayed one night in the Amphone-guesthouse of Attapeu.

On the 2nd of April we left Attapeu at 6.00h for Pakxong which we reached 8:45h.We met Mr. Bualay from the Cultural Office of Pakxong and we spoke to the Mayor of Pakxong about our working tasks. Then we picked up Mr. Uthay in Pakse and went with him and Mr. Bualay to Ban Chatsan. Ban Chatsan is a 2-year old resettled village of the Jaheun-Minority.We recorded a singer, a khen-player and gong-player. After that, we went to Ban Namtang of the Laveng-Minority. There was a wedding party and we found 3 musicians who played in the same arrangement as the Jaheun but a completely different repertoire. We left Ban Namtang at 17:45h for Pakxong and had dinner together with our two local advisors. We stayed in a guesthouse that was formerly the residence of the GDR experts.

On the 3rd of April we visited together with Mr. Bualay and Mr. Uthay two villages and made arrangements for two days later after our return from Sekong. At 10.30 we left Pakxong for Sekong which we reached at 12.00h.

After lunch we visited the Department of Information and Culture. We met Mr. Sivilay, the head of the Department, who informed us about the present situation in the province of Sekong. We found a place to stay in the back of a Vietnamese restaurant. In the afternoon we searched for musicians near Sekong and made an appointment for the evening. After dinner we went back to Ban Mo where 2 musicians of the Alak-Minority waited for us. There was one gong-player that played a wonderful solo. A khen-player accompanied him as a singer of an old legend.

After that we went to Ban Nonnongva of the Kalieng-Minority and we recorded about 50 people that prepared all their different performances in a short time for us. We finished this very successful working day about 23.00h.

The next morning we went to Ban Kandon Mai of the Katu-Minority that was rehabilitated after the people left the old village in 1995. We recorded about 25 musicians and dancers. There we found some interesting musical instruments as the fiddle so pak (kony) and a transverse flute with one central blowing hole and no finger holes.

We bought this instrument for presentation. After lunch together with the musicians we returned to Sekong. In the evening we observed the preparation of further performance. On the 5th of April we recorded these prepared performances of the Kalieng- and the Nghe-Minority near the Sekong River. It was very hot and noises from the ferry disturbed some times. So we finished our work after 12.00h and reported to the Department of Information and Culture about our outcomes in the province of Sekong. After that we went back to Pakxong and picked up Mr. Bualay. We went together to the village of the Lave-Minority (Brau of the Boloven-Plateau), which we had already visited 3 days before. Because of very heavy rain coming down the mountains we had to wait an hour.

Then we recorded their gong ensemble, the pair of flat gongs and two lullabies. At 16.30h we went back to Pakxong and spent the evening together with Mr. Bualay.

On the 6th of April we went to Pakse and to township of Champassak crossing the Mekong by ferry. There we met Mr. Ta who invited us to visit Wat Phou. It was the first day without recording appointments and we enjoyed the tour. After lunch we stopped for a short talk to the musicians of Champassak whom we already met in February 2000. Then we returned to Pakse and rested in a guesthouse. In the late afternoon we checked the car again and repaired it where necessary. The next day we went to Ban Nanong in the province of Salavan and met some families that lived here before 1975. The Taoi-Minority living near the village before was gone into the mountain area of the province. So we didn't find musicians. We continued our trip to Thakhek, which we reached at 15.30h.

We visited a cave and met some of the musicians we already recorded in July 2000. We gave them their photos and a copy of the recordings. We stayed in a guesthouse in Thakhek for one night and returned to Vientiane on the 8th of April, 2 days later as planned.

The results from this very well organized fieldtrip are excellent. We recorded 8 hrs of music on DAT, 5 hrs video on DV and took 144 photos. Our experience showed that it is preferable to work with local advisors more than with delegates from the Ministry of Information and Culture from Vientiane.

We found and recorded musical traditions from 12 different minorities of the South. The most serious cultural changes might happen to the Taoi and the Alak after resettlement.

On the first level of civilization we saw people in Lao Sekong with only a slim chance of a higher education. They opened up to information and gained external knowledge of what they could afford, and to have better access to electricity and modern communication technologies.

On the second level we were surprised at the proportion of people living below the consumption poverty line, which is smaller than in the well-educated districts on the Vietnamese side in Kontum, Pleiku and Gia Lam. Also in other parts of the Mekong community we observed an asymmetrical development of education and poverty that works for a more or less better reception of innovative structures. The social pressure is less, thanks to the better natural environment. So, the chances of accessing people through the accessibility of audiovisual documents are quite good, and we hope to see the living conditions improving.

* * *

Now let us view the other side of the world: Students at German universities. We can presuppose the third level of civilization: 'to eat a certain quality of food'. Behind the depressing statements above, we found serious questions. The ideas of access to related topics in audiovisual documents are completely different. I used a few of the wonderful examples in the range of activities that correspond to the long-distance online course INF 430 of the Charles Stuart University NSW, recommended and supported by ScreenSound Australia and the SEAPAVAA.

Figure 5: Students of the Johann Wolfgang Goethe University on excursion to the Deutsches Rundfunkarchiv in Wiesbaden organized by Anke Leenings.

Temporarily working conditions of this institution seem to be more stable as their own living conditions as students. The following examples were selected from e-learning papers produced by the students. The first topic dealt with access issues and there was an example of a television audiovisual archive that did not allow access. The question was: Would you find this a satisfactory response if you were a potential user who had been refused access? Explain why, or why not.[33]

---

[33] Original text of the activity: Television station XYZ has a large in-house collection of news items stretching back about thirty years, a range of documentaries and current affairs programs covering many important issues and events, and a large inventory of entertainment programs and soap operas featuring well known personalities which have repeat potential. The collection has considerable cultural and historical value and is a potentially rich source of material for media students and

Comments included:

1. If I were a potential user who had been refused access to the collection, I would not find this satisfactory because it does not explain why access to the collection is not permitted. If the TV station, as management says, has to manage the collection for the benefit of its shareholders, why not allow access by charging a fee?

2. The broadcasting station does not understand its cultural function.

3. Nobody can deny access to a collection for the reason that it is connected to private expenses. If public interest would demand access to the collection, then a state institution should decide whether they could support public accessibility and realise access to the collection.

4. If access to the collection is as limited as in this example, the question arises whether the collection could be managed through outsourcing the collection 'to the benefit of its shareholders'.

Nevertheless, further discussions on the relation between access and democracy show that Central European students know the shadow side of unlimited access.

The demands of differentiation between scholars, students, and scientists on one hand, and 'improvable interested people', alternate-

---

historians as well as program producers. However, station policy is to limit access to its own staff or to people working at the station on contract. There is no publicly-available catalogue, and the station's retention and preservation policies are only for internal use. The management responds to outside demand by saying that they are a business operation which cannot afford to provide a free or uneconomic public access service, and that the collection is a corporate asset which the station must manage - like its other assets - for the benefit of its share-holders. (see: INF 430 of the Charles Sturt University NSW, recommended and supported by ScreenSound Australia and the SEAPAVAA, Topic I, activities).

vely suspicious people, on the other, contradict their understanding of democracy. Therefore it seems to be unavoidable that our world society will be divided subsequently on a higher level again: into those who know and those who do not know; finally into doers and non-doers. Information through audiovisual documents becomes first of all a tool of power and imagination, as we have seen by the opening of the archives about Holocaust victims a long time after all the archives on the former GDR administration had been opened.

CONCLUSION

My brief discussion about the actually experienced media philosophy in administration at German universities and neighboring institutions, including organisations of students and the social reality in the centre of Europe, should offer a differentiated view on culturally influenced decisions on accessibility of audiovisual material.

We know that the purpose of all the work undertaken in an audiovisual archive is access. There is no point in keeping an audiovisual document unless there is an expectation that it will be used, either now or in the future.

However, rarely do we have the opportunity to discuss the opposite side: How do we access people through accessibility of these documents?

Finally, this mission seems to be the main challenge, which should be one of the most important intentions in the field of training and education. Therefore, I tend to prefer curricula in audiovisual archiving that include philosophical matters in a well-balanced way to support the very necessary ability to clarify decisions based on a kind of 'holistic' knowledge. It seems that education will always be under construction, therefore let us from time to time delve deeper into the basics of our work to make sure that we are not lost between the overwhelming power of technological and financial needs.

TEACHING FUTURE SPECIALISTS IN 'POPULAR MUSIC & MEDIA' REPORT ON AN EXPERIMENT AT THE UNIVERSITY OF PADERBORN[34]

What does a future specialist in popular music and media have to know about AV archiving? That was the main question I dealt with last year when I was invited to teach 'something with AV archiving'. When the newly installed Bachelor discipline in Popular Music and Media at the University of Paderborn did not get enough offers in the area of Media Practice, the administration remembered that besides my ethnomusicological studies I could present something on my AV experience, whatever it meant to them.

Figure 1: Students of Popular Music and Media in Paderborn.

---

[34] Jähnichen, Gisa (2005). Teaching future specialists on Popular Music & Media in AV-Archiving: Report on an experiment at the University of Paderborn. IASA Journal, 27, 66-72.

I took the opportunity to transform the lessons into an open offer to all the staff of the university who were interested, and finally 14 members found their way every week, on a Tuesday morning from 9 to I I, and were given a big package of homework each time.

Altogether I had 92 students and 14 colleagues in the class. The university campus is well equipped with teaching facilities; it has a good library, and a media section with Internet access and AV teaching material.

TEACHING MATERIAL AND READINGS
Preparing the lessons I also used IASA material, especially that of the Technical Committee.

But the main source was Ray Edmondson's Philosophy of AV Archiving and selected material from the Charles Stuart University, which offered a distance course, and together with Ray Edmondson and other colleagues engaged in SEAPAVAA developed very useful training material. Imo this material I incorporated the activities, wonderful examples of real problems in AV archive-related work. Construction of the lessons also more or less followed the basic course:

- History of the audiovisual media
- Exploring the audiovisual media in the global context
- Classic functions of an audiovisual archive
- Philosophical and ethical issues
- Legal issues in context
- Management and strategic thinking
- Politics and promotion
- Present and future realities

If we look at this curriculum we do not find anything unusual, but during the teaching processes very good discussions emerged, above all discussions about ethics of preservation and the main objective, access to AV material.

I Ethics of preservation
II Main aim: Access

Out of 92 students, 88 were very successful and scored more than 85%. This was mostly thanks to the well organised changes and interesting topics offered to the students, who at first were quite frustrated with dry archive material, but later opened themselves to the subject. In the final questionnaire, they explained that .. .' the subject 'AV-Archiving'was interesting owing to its ...

1. connection to all kinds of media
2. relevance to further musical creativity
3. political impact on different cultures
4. role as an indicator of cultural consciousness
5. complexity in dealing with the material and with different people

Nevertheless, there were a few discussions that were interesting to both popular music and media students. They discussed conflicts that are important and relevant to the music industry and to modern AV archives.

CONFLICTS

The popular music industry can be successful only when the cycle of creating-promoting-distributing a new pop song becomes faster and faster. How fast do we store these productions? How often will the whole 'item' be effectively used?

The songs must be technically more perfect and at the same time quickly forgettable to make the customer's head free to receive the next new pop song. Archiving seems to be counter-productive.

Song makers, producers, soloists, technicians and the music industry are in a profound dependence on each other. Archiving has to solve many contradictory problems, and has to do with politics, too. Do we want to be involved?

Finally, all the theories and discussions are useless if there is no way to translate the newly implemented knowledge into practice. Thanks to many colleagues, it was possible to set up media placements, for example in the following internships round the world:

- Svenskt Visarkiv Stockholm, The Centre for Swedish Folk Music and Jazz Research
- New Zealand Sound Archive, Christchurch
- Norwegian Institute of Recorded Sound, Stavanger
- National Library of Laos, Media Section,Vientiane
- Gramophone Records Museum and Research Centre of Ghana, Cape Coast
- Discoteca di Stato e Museo dell'Audiovisivo, Roma
- SWR,Abteilung Musikdokumentation, Baden-Baden

EXAMPLES

<u>New Zealand Sound Archive, Christchurch:</u>

Anna Wahdat had the opportunity to work at the New Zealand Sound Archive with Rachel Lord and her staff. She learnt a lot about social skills in an archive, an experience she had never counted as necessary before; she learnt about dealing with complicated ethical issues concerning minorities, and last but not least about the patience one should have while working with the material. An article about Anna appeared in a local newspaper:

Figure 2: Anna Wahdat.

Discoteca di Stato e Museo dell' Audiovisivo, Roma:

Florian Schmuck, a very shy, quiet student in class was working with different people in the Discoteca di Stato in Rome. In his final months he was involved in the issuing of recordings made by the local broadcasting RAI in the fifties. He said: "Fascinating and extraordinarily interesting was the edition of Sinatra's early recordings .. ."

The main motivation he got from a deep feeling for history and the responsibility for the image of history among the public, something he always forgot while dealing with charts and hits of popular music. Now, he is very proud to be named on the cover of those editions.

Fiure 3: An old recording of Sinatra; Figure 4: A new edition of the Discoteca di Stato, Rome.

<u>National Library in Vientiane, Laos:</u>

Two other students, two of the rare female students in that discipline, Denise Schneider and Beatrice Winter, did their media placement at the National library in Vientiane, Laos. They made researches into popular music in the capital and its surrounding areas; they started a new kind of collection and founded a new section of the archive: 'Lao Popular Music'.

Figure 5: Beatrice Winter and Denise Schneider at Wattay airport in Vientiane.

114

Everybody who knows the history and the present status of that country will agree that it is a very good idea, and a necessary one. We always pay attention to music productions of the past, the masterpieces of former generations, and we tend to forget that right now new music is being created and will be in great danger because it cannot compete with other mainstream productions on the world market. Creating modern music can be important to the identity of people in the same strong way as classic traditions. So, both students at least opened the minds of the present administration of the National Library.

One of their outcomes was the abstraction that 'you do not necessarily have to love the subject of collecting if you know enough about its importance and impact on the future'.

<u>SWR, Baden-Baden, Germany:</u>

Three other students, Victoria Kuszpa, Daniel Bonanati and Marc Enkhardt, did their practical work at the SWR,Abteilung Musikdokumentation, in Baden-Baden.

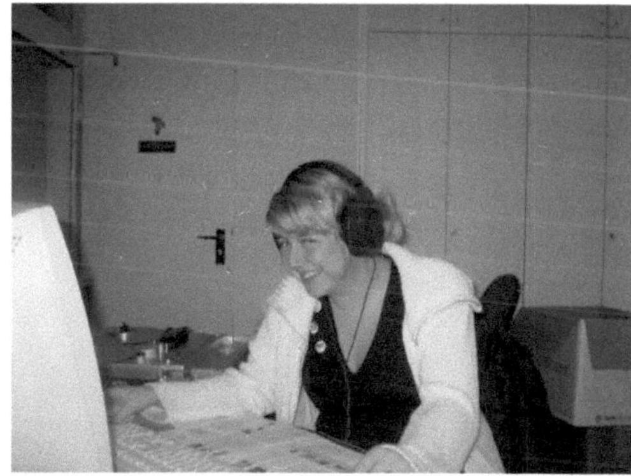

**Figure 6: Daniel Bonanati, Marc Enkhardt in the SWR, Baden-Baden;
Figure 7: Viktoria Kuszpa in the SWR, Baden-Baden**

They were very busy with the description of incoming items and with researches on request.

Concerning the classification of musical characters they developed a special critical view:

'it is hard to believe that the same descriptions will survive ourselves', they complained. As specialists in that special field of popular music they wanted to create more detailed and more flexible patterns, which would be more useful for programme makers. So, they explored the audiovisual being in its full sense as a soul that is always searching for a body, but can change the body whenever necessary and be in different bodies at the same time. too. Time and space are going to become other dimensions as before digital times. Their main outcome was philosophical ideas on AV works.

<u>Grammophone Records Museum and Research Centre of Ghana. Cape Coast:</u>

Not everything can have the same good beginning, so for example was the internship of the six young men: Cornelius de Haas, Moritz Gross, Finn Hassold. Tobias Vogel, Jochen Haeussler and Thorben Tietze at the Grammophone Records Museum and Research Centre of Ghana. Cape Coast. They found very interesting surroundings and were highly motivated, but the storage conditions was not ideal and although they were willing to help with any kind of work, it did not seem that solutions were wanted.

Figure 8: Reality behind the curtain - a storage room in the institution in Cape Coast, Ghana.

116

As you may remember, I first wrote a letter via the IASA listserv to all members, requesting media placements; that we were well trained students who were interested in all kinds of dealing with media and AV material. The first response came from the Cape Coast. However, the Museum told us soon after that costs of the attachments and the apprenticeship will be problematic. The six students, interested in this internship, could not be employed full time in the little museum. The Museum suggested some courses to be organized in addition to the main work in the museum.

The undertaking began on time in September. The first month went well although not all scheduled courses took place, the digitisation in the museum did not start, and one student returned for health reasons.

Figure 9: Paper sleeves ordered by the German intern Jochen Häußler.

By the second month 30% of the promised courses had not yet started; the work at the museum did not start, except for some

117

renaming of files with the file maker programme the students had brought with them. The students were concerned about the hopeless situation and ordered record covers on their own, hoping that they would have the chance to contribute at least something. But none of the interesting recordings could be heard because the amplifier was broken and the director refused to make use of the computer.

Two months after the students arrived they had not yet received any invoice or receipt for their expenses. The teachers also complained about not being paid in full. Only 15% of the course fees reached the right persons. The private house where the students stayed had been rented for 10% of the so-called 'discount price'.

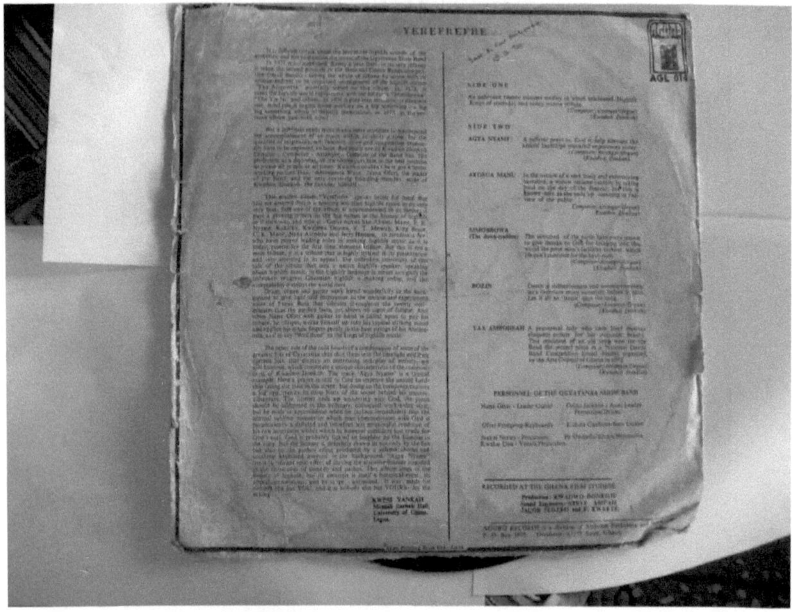

Figure 10: One of the rare Highlife-Covers - MMOBROWA (The wretched of the earth have every reason to give thanks to God for bringing into this world the poor man's facilities without which life can't continue for the have-nots (Composer/Arranger/Organ: Kwadwo Donkoh); AGL 014 <agard> 1975, "Yerefrefre" Ogyatanaa Show Band.

118

Nevertheless, the students learnt a lot. They were searching for other ways to get in touch with culture and modern media in Ghana. The students from Cape Coast experienced the full meaning, under complicated circumstances, of the four main tasks: collection development, preservation, collection management, and especially 'access'. They all could share their experiences with the other students and pointed out the main qualities of modern archivists as cultural consciousness, networking with international organisations and long term thinking. It was an important step to master conflicts and to find a way to solve problems.

The lessons given at the University of Paderborn helped them to intensify their practical skills and their theoretical knowledge. The colleagues at the university benefited from the whole course together with the students who brought their international experience into the discussion, and they implemented some of the ideas in their departments. They are now conscientiously following the actual development of technical and archiving standards. Somehow they feel that: IASA is watching you! Even that can sound good.

*** All the Photographs and other pictures were taken by the students or their supervisors who allowed them to use the material for this publication.**

ARCHIVES OF TRADITIONAL MUSIC IN LAOS (ATML)[35]

INTRODUCTION

Cultures consist of all kinds of historically developed skills of self-expression and self-presentation which are continuously changing. As a part of culture, tradition is responsible for the stability and continuity of a culture and is therefore a very sensitive issue in every society. Necessary social changes may renew traditions. In Laos the high speed of change at the present time is caused by different influences and could destroy the people's basic relationship to all kinds of traditions, particularly orally transmitted ones like music and dance. These two components of tradition are not to be compared with architecture or written literature. Sounding air or moving bodies cannot be stored somewhere for future use. When traditions are weakened or even destroyed, the orally transmitted arts are among the first to be affected. Certainly, the majority of the younger generation, particularly those living in urban centers, is on its way to losing a historical understanding of traditional music and dance. Sooner or later, young people will forget the creative power of their own music and dance traditions and thus will lose a very essential part of their identity.

As a result, both the younger generation as well as the traditional musician may well be displaced and forgotten in the future. They need our help. The most effective way to preserve sound carriers is the establishment of archives of traditional music in which all music and dance practices are collected, documented, stored and prepared for public use. These archives should be accessible to all who are interested. At the same time, all sound and picture materials must be authorized to protect the rights of the performing musicians and dancers.

---

[35] First published: Jähnichen (2002). The Archives of Traditional Music in Laos. *100th Anniversary of the Berlin Phonogramm-Archiv.* Ed. by Gabriele Berlin und Artur Simon. Berlin: Ethnologisches Museum, SMPK, 330-340.

120

The Archives of Traditional Music in Laos, which were initiated by the University of Applied Sciences in Emden (Fachhochschule Oldenburg-Ostfriesland-Wilhelmshaven), Germany, and the Ministry of Information and Culture of Laos, are located at the National Library in Vientiane. The German Association for Technical Development Cooperation (GTZ) and the German Research Association (DFG) funded this project. Support came from the Berlin Phonogramm-Archiv as well, which is storing an entire set of all recordings under ideal conditions as well as offering practical advice concerning many technical tasks.

MAIN RESPONSIBILITIES

First, research requires methodological knowledge based on the internal systematization of traditional music in Laos. This means that we attempt to create a flexible classification system for music practices, which is applicable to each social and ethnic group living in Laos. In this endeavor, we must focus on the social and cultural contexts of music practices and terminology. For instance, the "performance of music" means different things in different cultural spheres; sometimes there is no word for "professional" or for "artistic" because the people do not make this distinction. On the other hand, they may make other kinds of distinctions, such as different specifications for each generation, for male and female, and so on. The following types of research were thus needed as a basic first step: collecting, archiving and analyzing of music; classifying repertoires; transcription of examples; and description of musical instruments and ensemble arrangements.

The second step was the development of the National Library's scientific resources by establishing and supporting a new department called the "Archives of Traditional Music in Laos," with its own systematization. This includes well-organized services such as a systematic musicological database on various media and a music library with a wide selection of books, both to be used for research and educational and public purposes. A very important task of the archives is to authorize collections and other scientific materials about music and to preserve the rights of the musicians and collectors through controlled public access.

The third step involves training and motivating the specially trained local staff to continue the culturally vital duty of documenting and preserving traditional music in Laos. This staff is trained in all basic scientific methodologies, technical knowledge and service skills.

ACTUAL WORKING CONDITIONS

The National Library in Vientiane is an old French building (formerly a police department) with two floors. The rooms where the archives have been established are on the second floor. The main working and storage room has no window, the light coming indirectly from the neighboring small room, which is closely connected through an open door frame, and from the lobby side, through glass doors (fig 1).

1   Office workstation
2 Audio workstation
3 Archiving computer
4 Video workstation
5 Main storing board
6 Library
7 Storage cupboard for blank materials
8 User area
9 Sanitary room

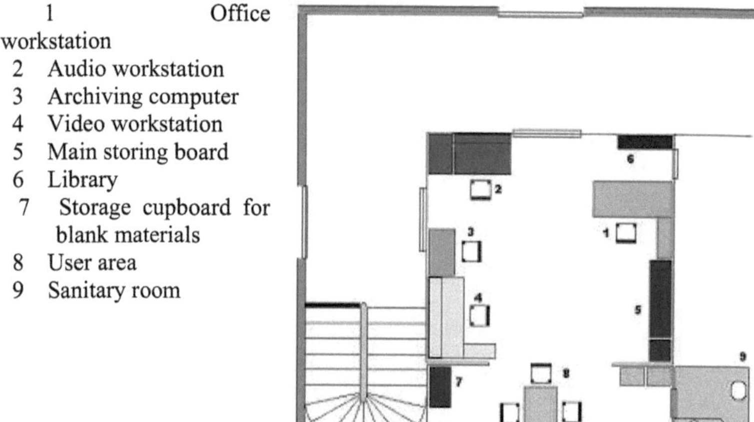

Figure 1: Layout of the Archives of Traditional Music in Laos at the National Library in Vientiane.

The temperatures vary between 16°C in winter and 35°C in April and October, and the humidity ranges from 86 to 99%, depending on the season, dry or rainy.

In the first 3 years, the original air conditioner was a very old one from Russia and mostly not in use. Instead, we usually switched on the big Chinese fan. Besides the oscillations in temperature and humidity, the continual presence of dust was a basic problem. Because of the humidity, we needed to open the windows and/or doors, but when we did so, we had to fight with layers of dust every day.

In this way, the problems associated with storing the tapes and protecting the equipment were related. In the beginning, we considered the usual assumption that archives need to have heavy metal boards with glass doors and safety locks to ensure the future existence of our recordings. Bad storage practices naturally mean lost material. After some experiments we found a very easy, cheap and effective way for protecting the tapes and smaller components of equipment: we bought a wooden storage cupboard with front doors made of willow wickerwork, which naturally absorbs humidity. One can observe everywhere, in markets or in households, how people use willow wickerwork baskets for storing and drying goods (fig. 2).

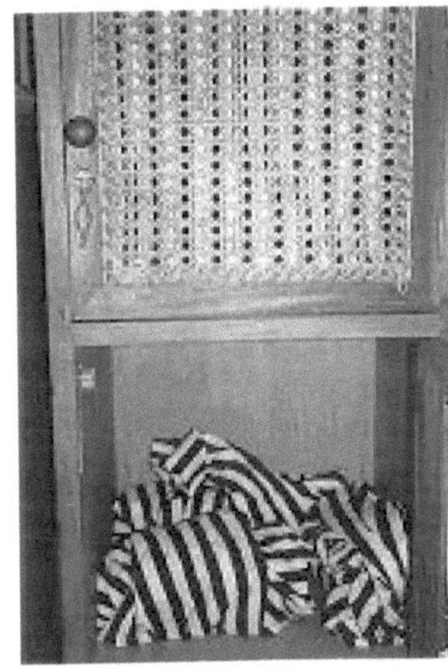

Figure 2: Section of storage board.

We made small holes in the back of the upper part of each section of storage cupboard; when a tea candle set inside did not burn continuously, we felt assured that the air would circulate throughout the cupboard. We put the tapes into bright, washable cotton bags, using the same material to wainscot the wickerwork doors inside the cupboard. The wainscoting is easy to change and wash, so we always have a relatively dry storage cupboard that is nearly free of dust. Of course, we did not forget to install some safety locks for our psychological peace of mind.

Finally and with the help of good friends, we got a modern air conditioner with an integrated dehumidifying unit. Thus, in combination with our "basket-storing" principles we improved the dust management enormously.

To protect the storage cupboard from insects, we use a special kind of chalk around the bottom of it. This chalk is made in Vietnam and has been successfully used for a long time. It is made of a natural base without aggressive chemical components. The audio equipment, which has to be cleaned once a week, is covered with bright cotton skirts, and not the black artificial leather cover with which it was delivered.

INTENTIONS OF COLLECTING AND DOCUMENTING

The archives deal with three kinds of material:

- "First grade collections": the collector is the owner of the recording equipment, the recorded material and the producer of the recordings. This kind of collection contains originals only.
- "Second grade collections": the collector is the owner of the recorded material, but is not the owner of the recording equipment and nor the producer. This contains a mixture of originals and copies.
- "Paid-for material": already published material, which we handle like originals.

124

All formats of sound material coming in have to be archived first on DAT (digital audio tapes). Each title receives a code number, which is its main reference; all other items such as transcriptions, instrumental descriptions, photos, illustrations, video movies and others are arranged according to this code number (figs. 3–5).

Fig. 3: Thongbang Homsombat works with video recordings; Fig. 4. Bounmy Phonsavanh transcribes lyrics of songs and completes data entries.

Fig. 5: Before transcribing the music, the tuning of the strings must be checked.

From these security copies we make user copies on DAT. Additionally, we produce analogue copies on cassettes tapes. We thus store one title four times, which are named: Original, Safety, Master, and Analogue. While producing the safety copies, all data are noted on data sheets (we use Access databases). After that, a copy of the complete sound and video material is archived in the "Berliner Phonogramm-Archiv" at the Museum of Ethnology in Berlin-Dahlem, Germany. Safety copies are stored in a special room (15°C, less than 25% humidity) and user copies are codified according to the system in the Archives (the so-called 'M-numbers'). From every collection we choose some examples for musical transcription, write descriptions of musical instruments and file photos and video recordings in relation to the code numbers. Finally, we prepare scientific reports, copy the recordings once more for the musicians and send them some photos as well.

CONTRACT FORMS

Contract between the Archives of Traditional Music in Laos and the COLLECTOR

1.   The ATML is responsible for the archiving of all kinds of material that belongs to the collection. Archiving collates the production of a digital safety copy, a digital user copy, an analogue copy and one backup copy, which will be sent to the Berlin Phonogramm-Archiv, Germany. Additionally there will be stored copies or originals of pictures, photos and drawings, written documents and any other material belonging to the given collection.

2.   The ATML insures that the edition of code numbers for each title and item protects the rights of the collector and the recorded musicians, singers and other individuals. In the case of commercial use of one or more of these authorized titles or items, the COLLECTOR has to agree in written form and should include his/her conditions.

3.   The ATML is responsible for the careful storage of the collection. In case of loss or damage, the ATML has to provide the reconstruction from the backup copy, which is archived in the Berlin Phonogramm-Archiv, Germany.

4.   The COLLECTOR has to contribute all information about the recordings and the other items, including necessary agreements between the musicians, singers or other individuals with the named collector in case of commercial use.

5.   The COLLECTOR has the right to get a complete digital or analogue copy of his material including the accompanying documentation made by the ATML.

6.   The COLLECTOR should inform the ATML about editions made by other institutions such as archives, broadcasting and any form of public usage.

7.   The COLLECTOR agrees with the public access to his/her collection except for commercial use.

Contract Between the ATML (Archives of Traditional Music in Laos) and the USER

1.   The ATML allows the copying of titles or items (documentation, pictures, drawings, photos and other written material) with the following code-number:

Code-number	Format

2.   The USER is committed to protect the rights of the collectors, musicians and other individuals concerning these titles or items. It is forbidden to make additional copies of these titles or items without the actual agreement of the responsible collector. Commercial use is not allowed at all.

3.   The USER has to pay for the tape material and a service fee according to the total amount of copies.

TECHNICAL EQUIPMENT

For sound archiving we use two digital audio tape recorders, one high-quality cassette recorder, a double tape recorder, a record player with amplifier, a CD player and a 16-channel Mackie-Mixer. In the video section we work with two S-VHS-recorders, a cheap title generator, a mixer and two multi-system screens. Of course, a digital cutting unit would be good to have but, compared to other projects in Laos, our small project is not wallowing in money. For the stationary equipment in Vientiane we work with a good voltage stabilizer.

The equipment for field research consists of a digital audio tape recorder, a professional cassette recorder, one digital video camera, which functions with Hi8 tapes (all from Sony), two mono microphones (Sennheiser MD 425) and one Beyerdynamic stereo microphone, and one photo camera (Canon EOS 300). Best for our purposes is light equipment with a large capacity and minimal requirements in energy. Because of the very desolate conditions of the roads in some areas of Laos, we often have to walk long distances and operate without electricity.

One of the future services of the Archives will be the possibility for recordists to borrow recording equipment from us under the condition that we receive a complete copy of the recorded materials.

DATA ENTRIES

The first data are to be written onto a form while recording and should be checked, if possible, by the musicians. We use Access forms for the final entries when we are copying with code-writing (S-copies).

Up to June 2002 we processed 32 collections from 26 different ethnic groups. The amount of recordings reached 1163 on 106 original data carriers such as DAT, MC, Hi8, DV8, VHS, S-VHS and CD, and the duration of music we have recorded is 114 hrs, 32 min, 43 sec.

We edited the Research Report - ARCHIVES OF TRADITIONAL MUSIC IN LAOS / Lao-German Co-operation: Ministry of Information and Culture, National Library of Laos – FH Oldenburg-Ostfriesland-Wilhelmshaven, GTZ, DFG; Vientiane 1999 – 2001 (446 p., 90 fig., 89 photos, 135 musical transcriptions, 108 transcriptions of song lyrics); Editor: Gisa Jähnichen / Assistant Editors: Thongbang Homsombat, Bounmy Phonsavan, Duangmixay Likaya, Sonja E. Mezger; Editorial Office: ATML - National Library of Laos, Kongdeuane Nettavong, P.O.Box 122, Vientiane, Lao PDR/ Fachhochschule Oldenburg-Ostfriesland-Wilhelmshaven, Bereich Sozialwesen, Georg Rocholl, Constantiaplatz 4, 26723 Emden, Germany.

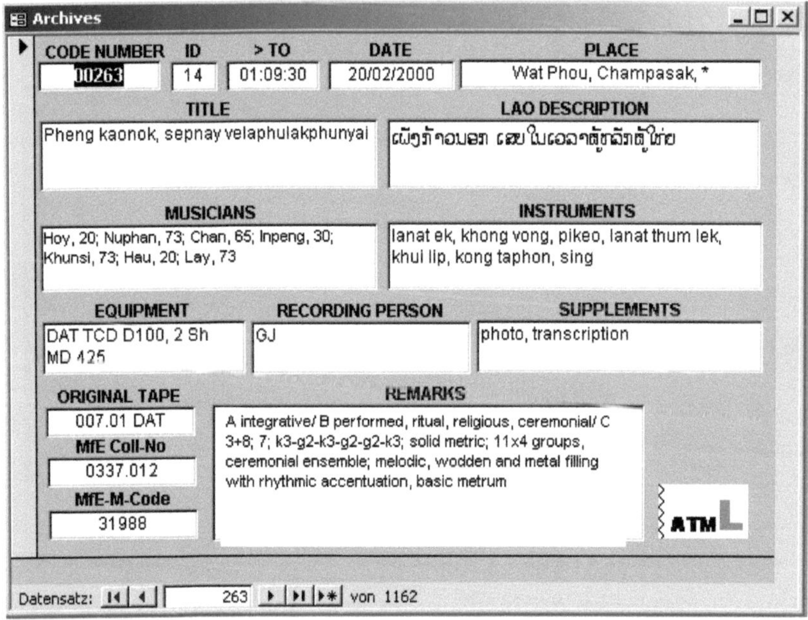

Figure 6: Database entry form. Sound recordings are the main reference. Other types of material are described as supplements.

In June 2002 we edited a study on khen playing and khen making with the title "Khen le Siangkhen" in Lao language that bases on our data entries and researches (Kongdeuane Nettavong: "Khen le

Siangkhen", ed. by Gisa Jaehnichen, ATML, Vientiane, 84 p., 9 fig., 13 photos and 12 musical transcriptions).

Khen playing is without doubt one of the essential parts of Lao musical traditions. Many people identify the sound of the khen with their native cultural expressions.

In the Archives of Traditional Music of Laos we collected 602 sound and video documents of khen playing and khen making. We learned that people living in Laos use different kinds of khen with different intentions and a great range of highly finished repertoires. Therefore, the whole phenomenon of khen playing in Laos has many images.

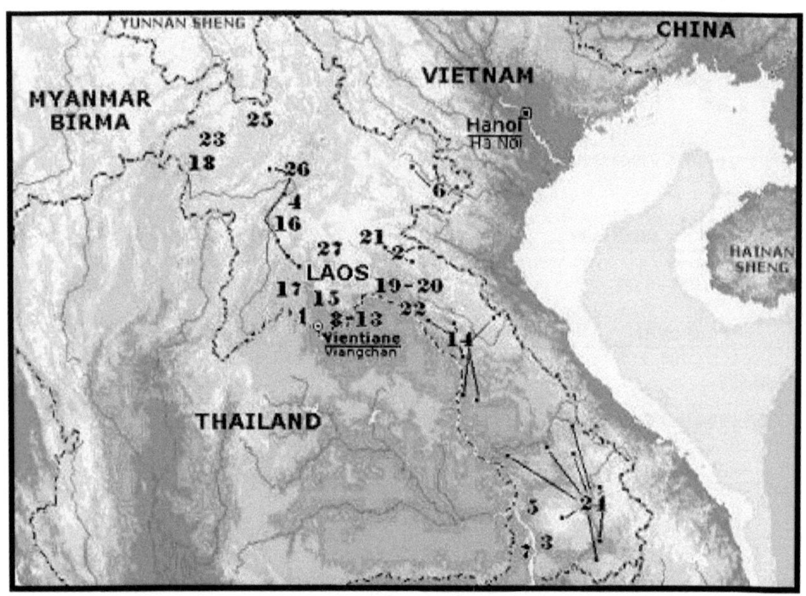

Figure 7: Field work destinations and reference number of collections made between May 1999 and April 2001.

On the other hand, to the young generation, especially in urban centers, which didn't have any chance to come in contact with traditional musical practice, the khen sounds undifferentiated as an antiquated musical instrument and is anticipated as a sign of cultural backwardness.

130

The first step to open their mind is to help them to understand the multifaceted culture of khen playing and the art of khen making in their own language. Now, using modern scientific methods, it is possible to make traditional musical culture accessible to many people with different backgrounds.

So, modernity and tradition do not except each other. They are both parts of our present life. The ATML-team with Kongdeuane Nettavong tried in this study to overcome this bias in a very successful way (from the editor's preface).

SYSTEMATIZING OF MUSIC PRACTICES

Usually societies on a less advanced level of cultural exchange (e.g., minorities without access to contemporary media) or on a more intense level of contact with cultures very different from their own (e.g., majority populations or those in urban areas) prefer to systematize musical activities according to the occasion. This systematizing takes place unconsciously and occurs with more accurate information according to the number of participants, the arrangement of musical instruments, song lyrics or other criteria.

In general, this kind of systematizing is accepted by the majority of each society, even if we have to consider differences among them related to the status and individual musical motivations of their members. A musician will recognize a single piece of music in a different way from a consumer of the same piece. For example, s/he will arrange her/his musical production from the practical viewpoint of making music. Some pieces are easy to perform while others cannot be memorized completely. So musicians learn to systematize their music practices according to the musical structures and then complete the system by comparing several occasions that demand these actual structures.

A few observations like these make it easy to understand why we have to go more deeply into the different relationships between socially conscious interpretation and individual experiences, aspects that overlap each other. We need to create a flexible and yet adequate overview that gives us room to treat the specific system of each culture.

Our research leads to the following basic dispositions:

A. Systemizing of musical activities according to the number of participants

B. Systemizing of musical activities according to the occasion

C. Systemizing of musical activities according to musical structures

A. SYSTEMATIZING OF MUSICAL ACTIVITIES ACCORDING TO THE NUMBER OF PARTICIPANTS

1. Individual (self-producing for self-listening)

The category 'Individual' means that the music is self-produced for self-listening. Thus, any kind of music that can be produced by one person can be placed in this category.

2. Dialogue (two persons or very small groups with pair-structures)

The condition of the category 'Dialogue' is the implemented opportunity for the development of two interrelated roles in music production. Included in this category are not only songs in a question-answer structure and other kinds of response singing but also instrumental music for interrelating instruments and singers accompanied by instruments.

3. Integrative (middle to large groups)

Even if it seems to be difficult to define this category, it is actually the most obvious one because of all the musical ensembles that are included in it. Here different musical roles can also be created, but the musical production does not necessarily have to bear an interrelating character. An example would be to play a set of instruments that we consider to be only one instrument (e.g., a set of bamboo tubes or gongs). The main intention is the production of one whole piece by many persons. The practice of 'dialogue' can be included in this category, but it does not dominate the creative process.

4.   Associated (the whole community)

The category 'Associated' mostly contains the repertory of the third category, especially the few less complicated pieces; these can be performed by anybody, since they do not require special musical skills. The main intention is the production of musical events for identification within the community.

5.   Interchanging (people from several communities)

Interchanging musical production means more or less an abstraction of traditional tunes that can be identified for more than one ethnicity or social group. Such trans-ethnic musical pieces and songs are mostly a part of newer regional or national musical activities. But some tunes highly typical of one ethnicity or region that have become widespread through traveling music groups or mass media can fall into this category as well.

B.   SYSTEMATIZING OF MUSICAL ACTIVITIES ACCORDING TO THE OCCASION

As the most practical scheme, we decided on the following order:

I.   Performed music

    A.   Ritual music
        1.   Musically structured praying declamations
        2.   Religiously determined music
        3.   Ceremonial music

B.   Entertainment music
         1.   Epic genres
         2.   Dance music
         3.   Instrumental entertainment
         4.   Dramatically determined music

II.   Utilized music
A.   Discrete songs / Discrete playing
B.   Playing songs
C.   Working songs
D.   Love songs
E.   Lullabies, songs for children

The different parts of this construction are not mutually exclusive, for example, a lullaby can also be classified as 'performed music' when played as dramatically determined music on stage. Or ritual declamation can fall into the category of 'discrete songs' under 'utilized music.' This categorization depends on the actual circumstances. When we classify our recordings, we take into consideration all possible circumstances because of the special side effect of the recording situation, which usually changes music with a performing character (or transformed ritual practices) into utilized situations.

C.   SYSTEMATIZING MUSICAL ACTIVITIES ACCORDING TO MUSICAL STRUCTURES

First, we analyze the construction of the musical material in terms of the periodic ambit and quantity of semantic patterns, which also includes stable pitch connections or different treatments of pitches. Then we study the interval relationships and hierarchies within those relationships. We call the basic pitch the 'related pitch' because of the appearance of different 'related pitches' belonging to the structure of the musical units. As long as we have not yet completed the study of the entire musical material of one particular musical culture, we avoid the fixing of tonal systems. That becomes the task for further research. But we can observe sonic hierarchies by using relative expressions.

Secondly, we study the structure of musical units in relation to the phrase structure and the serial structure. The phrase structure we divide into free metric, solid metric, mixed, and polymetric phrase structures. In our transcriptions we usually try to make these structures visible through the order of rows. The serial structures we divide into 'single-part' and 'multi-part.' In addition to these, we observe different combined structures, especially in complex performances.

Thirdly, we analyze the musical arrangement and its variability. We find variable arrangements but we also find pieces with invariance of sound color, sound volume, and of the performing person in terms of sex, age or special experiences. Finally, we try to comment on the categories of sound functions and their hierarchies. The result of the systematization according to this key form is accessible through the data entries in the section entitled 'Remarks'.

FUTURE OUTLOOK

Under the management of the Director of the National Library, Kongdeuane Nettavong, who is simultaneously the official head of the project, a team of three privately funded staff members works in the Archives of Traditional Music in Laos. During the past two years, Thongbang Homsombat has successfully completed the training units "Classification and archiving of sound material," "Audio engineering," "Instrumental sound production," "Video engineering" and "Transcription of sound documents." As the scientific and technical administrator of the archive, she is responsible for sound and video archiving as well as for the further training of the two other staff members and two new students. In the end, everyone has to be able to perform all the tasks of collecting, archiving and documenting sound recordings. Additionally, Bounmy

Phonsavanh, who is the secretary, is specialized in the transcription of song lyrics. All-round skills are obligatory at least to serve the public in an adequate way. The public interest is the greatest hope for the future of the Archives of Traditional Music in Laos and for the future of the central ideas that created it.

COLLECTING PRINCIPLES AND THEIR OBSTACLES - OR: HOW TO COLLECT "NOTHING"[36]

The Archives of Traditional Music in Laos, which were founded by the University of Applied Sciences in Emden (FH Oldenburg-Ostfriesland-Wilhelmshaven), Germany, and the Ministry of Information and Culture of Laos, are located at the National Library in Vientiane. The German Association for Technical Development Cooperation (GTZ), and the German Research Association (DFG) funded it. Support came from the Berliner Phonogramm Archiv as well, by way of storing a whole set of the recordings under ideal conditions and through practical advice on many technical tasks.

The worldwide accessible stock of recorded music of traditional Laotian music practices is very small in number. Therefore the first and most important task was the archiving and protection of recordings made in Laos, which were not accessible until today, and the collecting and documenting of music practices of the many different ethnicities living in the territory of present day Laos. After a few weeks of preparation, technical installation and training, our team was ready to apply the four key principles of collecting:

1. There are no uninteresting music practices
2. Everybody is capable of taking part in musical activities
3. In the course of our working and the discussions that take place about it, no one should evaluate the recordings or the recorded persons qualitatively; each recording and each person is of the same importance.
4. We make recordings of musical performances that are complete, with all repetitions: we do not edit or rearrange material to suit a later utilization.

---

[36] First published: Jähnichen, Gisa (2001). Collecting principles and their obstacles – or: How to collect nothing. *IASA Journal, 18,* 15-22.

On our field researches we took two different tasks into consideration. First we made so called point researches on significant occasions as New Year festivals, temple festivals or on prepared groups of musicians. Secondly, and that was the more difficult, we made broad researches, which were not announced in advance. These researches were to give us an overview about the currently existing music practices within an area.

Shortly after the beginning of our project we addressed some very serious questions: why are we so often confronted with the situation that in remote villages traditional musical life seems to be a secret? What do they understand by the terms 'traditional' and 'musical life'?

'Tradition' is actually a very multi-faceted term. These circumstances belong to the history of the country and with the people living in its territories. For the Lao majority the term can refer to inheritance (pheunmeuong) or custom (laodeum), and means old, native or simply Laotian. Only the most socialized communities as the Lao-Loum and their groups reflect customary practices as a part of their tradition, making practical distinctions between these and new habits that come generally from abroad.

The invention of traditions needs a consummation of the designed development of cultural skills and products, and it is a result of cultural comparison, too. This cultural comparison between the Lao-majority and the neighbouring countries is nowadays given by contact through different media and communication. But cultures far away and in autarchic living communities comprehend their old and inherited customs as present day activities. They do not recognise abstract notions of what is 'traditional' and what is 'modern'.

The differences in cultural development between the people living in the territory of present Laos are so tremendous that we find another important problem: the definition of these people and the definition of their relationships between each other. Ethnographical researches on this subject are at the very beginning. The number of different ethnic groups in Laos is usually given as sixty-three, but is not really provable. We accept as true that there are only forty-eight different

138

ethnic groups. Relatively isolated living groups with remarkable cultural signs as the Ta Oi, the Bru or the Laven, are easy to identify. More difficult is the definition of people that are subdivided into smaller cultural sub-groups such as the Iu Mien, the Hmong, the Khmu or the Thai. The most diversified group is that of the Lao. The reason for this is not only the relatively large number of inhabitants (nearly 50 % of the total), but also the history of their development. For many centuries the Lao have been in the habit of separating into settlements all over the country.

The Lao developed agriculture extensively and meant that they became dominant from the 13th century onwards. This dominance did not take the form of a permanent struggle to win territory but it did lead to the wide dispersal of their groups into many near-empty valleys and plains. The very good conditions in support of agricultural production slowed down the development of markets and townships, as was the case in other Southeast Asian countries since the beginning of the 16th century.

In this way the traditional culture of the Lao, until now, has many different local characteristics. From the Lao viewpoint, strict distinctions are made between their own groups. But all the other minorities living in the territory of Laos are usually classified, without any distinction, as one or other of two big cultural groups: the Lao Theung living on the slopes of the mountains, and the Lao Sun living on the tops of the mountains.[37] Perhaps, they do not like to be confused by historically derived differences between their diverse parts. Thus they mostly prefer a kind of simplicity that also implies the ignorance of the Lao majority, which sometimes - on the other hand - causes cultural opposition against Lao cultural values. It is obvious, therefore, that some minorities try to establish their own

---

[37] This classification into three groups: the Lao Loum (the ethnic Lao, living in the valleys), the Lao Theung (minorities living on the slopes of the mountains), and the Lao Sun (minorities living on the tops of the mountains), is only half a century old and was unfortunately created by a "Lao Sun", Toulia, who was a member of the first national parliament.

cultural values by fixing former changeable customs into something tradition-like.

That is where our problems began: What is the key process of establishing traditions in the given surroundings? The creating of something tradition-like is influenced by an interpretation of tradition as we can observe in many developing countries: the transformation of making music into finished music products, the transformation of an act into a thing.[38] What they understand by a finished music product is a representative performance, which summarises and selects from local practices and becomes a typified abstract or a cultural symbol. The manner of the product comes from the socially implicated idiom of performance: a stage, an introduction, an excerpt from an abstract tune, and may be a dramatically styled dance in uniform colourful dress with a performance highlight as a conclusion. In short, it represents another thing compared to their practical experience. Indeed, this process needs specialists who are experienced in summarizing and selecting through their social contacts to the Lao majority, and not every village has specialists of this kind.

On our field trips into the mountains one of the most widespread answers we heard was that "we make music, but we don't have anybody who performs it for you". In some villages we heard: "we know one song, but the only singer is absent / is sick". That means that they know about the common tendency of cultural representation, they believe that they know about the thing what we are looking for. They are ashamed of the fact that they are not able to serve us with their music product; they had not yet developed it. Therefore they had no thing or, simply, nothing. We explained many times that we were not seeking fixed symbols, that we were searching for living examples, for instance, how to make music, how to celebrate it, how to be happy. We were actually very interested in their nothings. So we reached a point where we were fighting against

---

[38] With another intention than John Blackings difference of ' music as process' and 'music as product' (see John Blacking. How musical is man? Seattle: University of Washington Press).

ourselves, because it was true that we had come to transform action into a thing, even if we had not intended to do so. The only way out was to demonstrate that we would not use the thing, in other words our recordings, arranged according to neutrally valued code-numbers, as their product. We focussed on the creativity of individuals or of small groups in order to obtain, step by step, a picture of the whole musical activity of a village, or of the desired minority in the area. So, we had to do the opposite of developing a thing: no summarizing, no selection, no symbolism - because the singular creativity of each member contributes to the many-sided whole of their musical culture. The thing that we did became a plurality of actions, an anti-performance.

Everybody was proud of saying "I'm archived!" In their eyes, it was not music that was now archived somewhere; they - the individuals - were archived! That was much better than being represented by the only official singer or by the one fixed performance of a few nominated representatives.

Have a look at these two examples:

Code No.	00601
ID	12
Date	28/08/2000
Place	Lak 8, Luang Prabang
Title	Tot (Khmu)
Musician	Phan, f. 40
Instruments	tot Khmu+ vocal inserts
Kind of singing	Khmu. Luang Prabang
Participants	inividual, dialogue
Occasion	utilized. discre te. playing, for children
Periodical ambit	decime
Quantity of semantic patterns	7
Interval relationship	mi3/ ma2/ mi3/ ma2/ ma2/ mi3[39]

---

[39] The abbreviations ma and mi stand for major and minor. These are rough terms for primary orientation used by local colleagues trained in Western music. They do not represent musical thoughts of the musicians.

Sonic Hierarchy	5
Phrase structures	free metric
Serial structures	phrases of diffe rent length
Arrangement	pi Khmu + female voice (Sound invariance)

Figure 1: Khmu-woman playing flute and simultaneously singing (the notation shows two lines).

Code No.	00180
ID	27
Date	09/01/2000
Place	Kho. Xamtai. Huaphan
Title	Khap uyphonkhekmajiam (Thai deng)
Musician	Thongsy, m. 46
Instruments/ Kind of singing	khap Thai deng
Participants	Thai deng, integrative

142

Occasion	performed. entertaining. epic / utilized, love song
Periodical ambit	none
Quantity of semantic patterns	8. 2 flexions
Interval relationship	ma2/ ma2/ mi2/ ma2/ ma2/ mi3/ ma2
Sonic Hierarchy	8. ma3
Phrase structures	free metric
Serial structures	phrases of different length (a+b b+a)
Sound invariance	male voice
Arrangement	singing

Figure 2: a Red-Thai-man with a bundle of leaves is singing a local tune of Sam Neua (the notation shows only one line).

As applied to this particular piece of research, the way in which we collected, as explained above, was very successful, even if I felt hypocritical about it at first. Our colleagues from the Ministry of Information and Culture and its local offices who accompanied us evidently did make differences between the recorded actions, between the different social statuses of the recorded persons, and they were not very patient. Through these experiences we learnt that our principles of collecting were right, but there were obstacles. We went with the intention of gathering traditional music of an ethnicity in its normal state but we found that many people had their own understanding of normality, which resulted from their individual history and conception of making music.

143

There were arguments about correctness. For example, we heard: 'The sister of this man is married to a Lao from Sukhuma, he plays the kachappi, but that is not our music".

Or:

"He plays the gong without respect to the night ghosts: we don't". These arguments about incorrect actions were just as interesting to us as all of our other documents. It was an actual reality that this person played the kachappi and this person did not respect the night ghosts. It was not up to us to decide whether it was correct or not, because we were not generating typical products: we were making recordings of individuals in action.

Some critics were concerned that we did not show enough responsibility for the image of the respective minorities, yet we did succeed, inadvertently, in capturing that second important thing, an image of a minority. Of the total amount of our recordings nearly 85 % were made for the first time. Moreover, we knew that everybody who took part had been recorded for the first and possibly for the last time, by any means. Next year, it would be another music/another thing. That is a lot of material on which to base an image and we used this to defend ourselves against the critics because we felt that there was no image, 'no thing', to be recorded. We made a cross-section of actual music practices; it was not our aim to record the whole musical history of a particular ethnic group. Place and time were determined. So we were able to defend ourselves, but we did start to think about why we made these recordings and what would be done after archiving.

We realized that when we take a first step, we have to take a second step as well. We have to try to describe, to study, to analyze the recordings, and that means that we have to create complementary things, which implicate their ethnic and social history through individual actions, and we have to return many times for further recordings. Otherwise we cannot protect the character of our collecting; we cannot prevent the things that the users of our archives

144

will create. This will be the urgent task of the near future and we need many interested colleagues to continue in this way.

The apparently harmless task of touching the recording button at the right time and in the right place caused a few conflicts with my previous scientific plans. I thought that I would have the rare opportunity to obtain material that I could systemize into repertoires, systems of ethnic connections that I could analyze and compare with other materials from the region. That was not, in itself, wrong, but it was not all. There was an additional necessary job; to find out how quickly or how slowly, how consented or how reserved the musical actions needed to be before they became things and what did this unavoidable process change in the creative conception of each individual activity. That was the challenge I shared with my Lao colleagues. Collecting music as we have done is much more difficult than collecting written documents, which are already things that are made for storing. By making recordings we brought the acts that we recorded to the same level as written documents, downwards or upwards, according to the actual viewpoint. And we should consider how many times this process has already occurred in the history of recorded sound!

Living in a society, where the socialization of things is developed to a state of near perfection, to the extent that it even governs the relations between human beings, I prefer an understanding of scientific responsibility as one that cares about the social actions involved. The two years of field researches in remote areas of Laos demonstrated that our collecting, as an activity, was ultimately more important to the people than the present results that are stored and well documented in the capital. The act of collecting mobilized them, made them proud and important. That seemed to be the main target and gave good reason for our undertaking. But it cannot be considered part of an evaluation system based on product quality that exists separate from time and place, separate from individual creativity. Therefore they are not comparable to our recordings from point researches.

The Present Situation

Under the management of the Director of the National Library, Kongdeuane Nettavong, who is simultaneously the official head of the project, a team of three privately funded staff members works in the Archives of Traditional Music in Laos. During the past two years, Thongbang Homsombat has successfully completed the training units Classification and archiving of sound material, Audio engineering, Instrumental sound production, Video engineering and Transcription of sound documents. As the scientific and technical administrator, she is responsible for sound and video archiving as well as for the further training of the other staff members. In the end, everyone has to be able to perform all the tasks of collecting, archiving and documenting sound recordings. Additionally, Bounmy Phonsavanh, who is the secretary, is a specialist in the transcription of song lyrics. Bouaket Saynyasan is a talented field trip organizer and an excellent off-road driver who is responsible for the basic documentation and technical support. All-round skills are obligatory at least to serve the public in an adequate way.

The public interest is the greatest hope for the future of the Archives of Traditional Music in Laos and for the future of the central ideas that created it. Therefore we developed a Service & Support Program that provides helpful opportunities for researchers and students as well as other interested people from abroad to step into the field of musical cultures in the territory of present Laos. As a government institution the Archives of Traditional Music in Laos can support (with modern office facilities including audio and video studio and field equipment. PC-workstations) field trip management including visa and other permissions and personal service for a very moderate charge, unlike in some other East Asian countries. On the other hand, the Laotian staff members will take part in these studies. they will open their scientific horizon from many different viewpoints and finally they will get a minimal income for further work until the Laotian government can afford these expenses. On behalf of my Laotian colleagues I invite all interested people to use this Service & Support Program.

Outcome (June 1999 - May 2001):
27 collections of 24 different ethnic groups
Audio: 992 recordings (78 hrs 42 min 49 sec) on 92 original items
Video: 1240 min
Photos: 692
Transcriptions: 135
Drawings: 70

REFERENCE

Jähnichen, Gisa (2001). Research Report — Archives of Traditional
    Music in Laos 1999-2001. Vientiane: National Library
    (ATML limited edition).